peter maggs

jenny quintana

move

pre-intermediate

coursebook

with CD-ROM

MACMILLAN

Contents map

Module 1 Vision

Unit	Topic	Language study	Vocabulary	Main skills
1 **I know what I like** pages 2–5	• Nature or nurture (three gifted young women) • Speed-dating	• Likes and dislikes, agreeing and disagreeing	• Phrasal verbs: growing up • Sports, leisure activities, types of film and styles of music	• **Reading:** understanding main informati • **Speaking:** discussing child development asking for and giving personal informatio • **Listening:** identifying key information
2 **Innovation** pages 6–9	• Great minds (Steve Jobs and Steve Wozniak, co-founders of Apple Computers) • Tokyo gizmo (innovative gadgets from a Japanese toymaker)	• Talking about past events (past simple and past continuous)	• *make* and *do*	• **Listening:** identifying main information • **Pronunciation:** regular past tense endings (*-ed*) • **Reading:** understanding main informati • **Speaking:** discussing the importance of inventions
3 **The sixth sense** pages 10–13	• Psychic powers • Your lying ways (sleeping positions)	• Expressing necessity and advice (*must(n't)*, *(don't) have to*, *should(n't)*, *ought to*, *don't need to*)	• Character adjectives	• **Reading:** understanding gist • **Writing:** an email to a friend • **Speaking:** discussing psychic powers; describing people • **Listening:** identifying particular information
4 **What do you do?** pages 14–17	• Any volunteers? (experiences of a volunteer working in China) • Volunteers needed	• Making promises, requests and predictions: *will*	• Work experience • Occupations	• **Reading:** identifying main information • **Listening:** identifying key information • **Speaking:** talking about jobs and career choices; making promises, requests and predictions

5 **Review unit** pages 18–21
• **Extra practice** pages 22–25 • **Grammar reference and wordlist** pages 26–28 • **Listening scripts:** pages 30–31 • **Communication activities:** pages 29, 32

Module 2 Taste

Unit	Topic	Language study	Vocabulary	Main skills
1 **Don't breathe a word!** pages 34–37	• Gossip • You didn't hear it from me	• Talking about recent events (past simple and present perfect simple) • Phrases to talk about time and quantity	• Phrases about friendship and rumour	• **Reading:** identifying key information • **Listening:** completing details of events • **Speaking:** listening and responding to news about other people
2 **Pass the popcorn, please** pages 38–41	• Mad about movies • Movie mistakes message board	• Asking for and giving opinions	• Types of film • Describing elements of a film	• **Reading:** identifying main ideas • **Listening:** identifying descriptions • **Pronunciation:** emphatic stress in description phrases • **Speaking:** discussing strengths and weaknesses of a film • **Writing:** a film review
3 **You must try it** pages 42–45	• A question of taste (response to blue food) • Good manners cost nothing (politeness in restaurant conversations) • Doing the right thing (cultural expectations)	• Quantifiers with countable and uncountable nouns	• Food • Ordering food in restaurants	• **Reading:** understanding main ideas • **Speaking:** roleplay between customer ar waiter; discussing good and bad manners • **Listening:** identifying correct informatic
4 **Followers of fashion** pages 46–49	• Looking good (beauty contest) • Body art	• Recognising and using phrasal verbs	• Describing appearance and things you wear	• **Reading:** identifying main ideas • **Speaking:** discussing beauty and body decoration • **Listening:** understanding descriptions of body art • **Writing:** an email explaining a decision

5 **Review unit** pages 50–53
• **Extra practice** pages 54–57 • **Grammar reference and wordlist** pages 58–60 • **Listening scripts:** pages 62–63 • **Communication activities:** pages 61, 64

Module 3 Motion

Unit	Topic	Language study	Vocabulary	Main skills
1 **Get down to the rhythm** pages 66–69	• Shake that thing (types and origins of music) • It's party time (festivals)	• *for* and *since* with the present perfect	• Types of music • Musical instruments	• **Reading:** ordering a text summary • **Speaking:** talking about music and festivals • **Pronunciation:** recognising strong and weak forms in sentences • **Listening:** identifying main information
2 **Just do it** pages 70–73	• Hit the streets (an unusual new sport: parkour) • Get moving (skating into work)	• Comparatives and superlatives	• *play, do, go* with sports and activities • Phrases with *get*	• **Listening:** understanding gist and identifying key information • **Speaking:** discussing sport and exercise • **Reading:** selecting an appropriate title • **Writing:** a short story with sequencers
3 **On the road again** pages 74–77	• Save our soles (three pilgrimage experiences) • Take a break (holidays)	• *say* and *tell* • Direct and indirect speech	• Prepositions of place • Words to describe location, accommodation and holiday activities	• **Reading:** understanding key details and summarising a story • **Listening:** identifying main information • **Speaking:** discussing travel and holiday preferences
4 **Out and about** pages 78–81	• Trouble in store (making complaints in shops) • What do I say? (shopping quiz)	• Talking about real and imaginary situations (first and second conditionals)	• Shopping vocabulary	• **Listening:** understanding mood and manner • **Reading:** understanding gist • **Writing:** a short dialogue • **Speaking:** buying and returning goods

5 **Review unit** pages 82–85
• **Extra practice** pages 86–89 • **Grammar reference and wordlist** pages 90–92 • **Listening scripts:** pages 94–95 • **Communication activities:** pages 93, 96
• **Use CD2 for listening activities in this module.**

CD-ROM

Location	• Modules 1–3, Units 1–4
Activities for each unit	• Language activity • Vocabulary activity • Common European Framework linked activity • Language game
Features	• Markbook – helps you to record and update your marks. • Bookmark – helps you to save your favourite activities. • Wordlist – helps you to create your own wordlists. • You can back up, restore and print out your Markbook, Bookmarks and Wordlists. You can also send saved files as emails. • For more information use the Help feature.

In the Coursebook:

three 32-page modules

On the CD-ROM:

48 language activities and games, a help section and markbook, wordlist and bookmark features

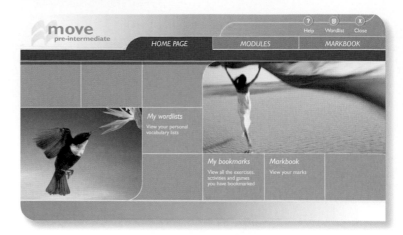

In each module:

four main units

a review unit

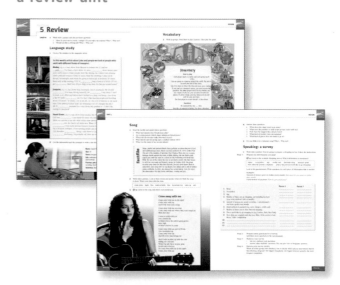

four extra practice pages

five reference pages: grammar, wordlist and listening scripts

two communication activity pages

Module 1
Vision

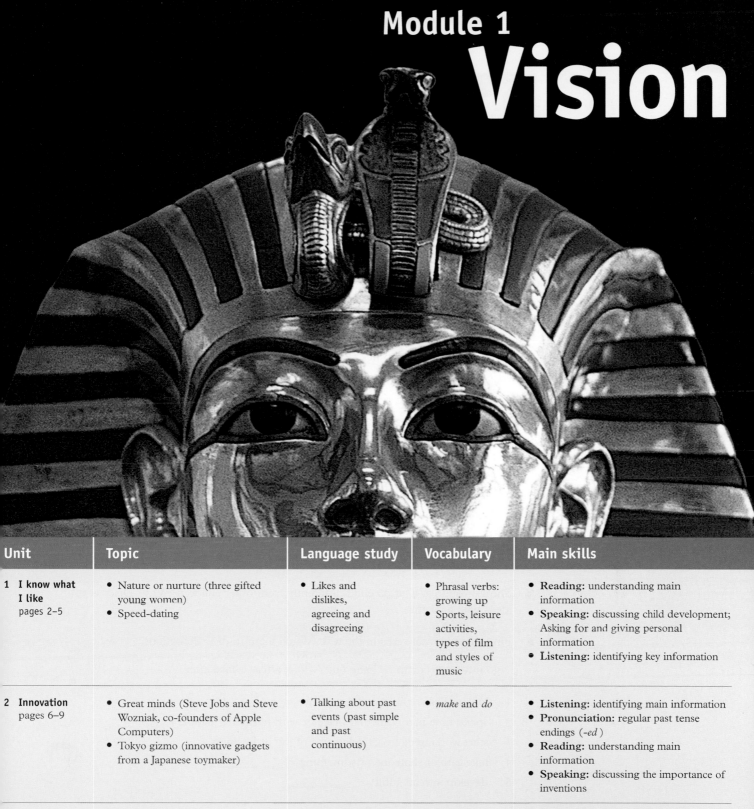

Unit	Topic	Language study	Vocabulary	Main skills
1 I know what I like pages 2–5	• Nature or nurture (three gifted young women) • Speed-dating	• Likes and dislikes, agreeing and disagreeing	• Phrasal verbs: growing up • Sports, leisure activities, types of film and styles of music	• **Reading:** understanding main information • **Speaking:** discussing child development; Asking for and giving personal information • **Listening:** identifying key information
2 Innovation pages 6–9	• Great minds (Steve Jobs and Steve Wozniak, co-founders of Apple Computers) • Tokyo gizmo (innovative gadgets from a Japanese toymaker)	• Talking about past events (past simple and past continuous)	• *make* and *do*	• **Listening:** identifying main information • **Pronunciation:** regular past tense endings (-ed) • **Reading:** understanding main information • **Speaking:** discussing the importance of inventions
3 The sixth sense pages 10–13	• Psychic powers • Your lying ways (sleeping positions)	• Expressing necessity and advice (*must(n't), (don't) have to, should(n't), ought to, don't need to*)	• Character adjectives	• **Reading:** understanding gist • **Writing:** an email to a friend • **Speaking:** discussing psychic powers; describing people • **Listening:** identifying particular information
4 What do you do? pages 14–17	• Any volunteers? (experiences of a volunteer working in China) • Volunteers needed	• Making promises, requests and predictions: *will*	• Work experience • Occupations	• **Reading:** identifying main information • **Listening:** identifying key information • **Speaking:** talking about jobs and career choices; making promises, requests and predictions

5 Review unit pages 18–21

• **Extra practice** pages 22–25 • **Grammar reference and wordlist** pages 26–28 • **Listening scripts:** pages 30–31 • **Communication activities:** pages 29, 32

1 I know what I like

LEARNING AIMS

- Can express likes and dislikes
- Can agree and disagree
- Can ask for and give personal information

Nature or nurture

Lead-in

1 Work in groups and discuss these questions.

1 Can you think of any people who became famous when they were young?
2 What are they famous for?
3 Are 'gifted' people born with talent or do they learn it?

Reading and vocabulary

1 01 Read the text about three gifted young people on page 3. What is each one's special talent?

2 Read the text again and tick (✓) the boxes that relate to each person.

		Flavia	Keira	Marla
1	She became famous before she was five.	☐	☐	☐
2	She left her country of origin when she was three.	☐	☐	☐
3	She knew what job she wanted to do when she was three.	☐	☐	☐
4	Her parents treated her normally.	☐	☐	☐
5	She continued her schoolwork while developing her talent.	☐	☐	☐
6	Her talent has made her rich.	☐	☐	☐

3 Should you treat a gifted child differently from other children? Why? Discuss your ideas with a partner.

4 Find these phrasal verbs in the text. Match them to their definitions.

go into   grow up   hang out   look after   take after

1 look or behave like an older relative = _____
2 spend time in a particular place or with particular people = _____
3 start working in a particular type of job or business = _____
4 take care of someone or something = _____
5 develop into an adult = _____

5 Complete these sentences using the phrasal verbs in Ex 4.
1 I think girls _____ more quickly than boys.
2 On Saturdays I usually _____ with my friends.
3 I would like to _____ the entertainment industry.
4 I always have to _____ my younger brother / sister.
5 I _____ my mother. We both have the same hair and eyes.

6 Work with a partner. Discuss the sentences in Ex 5. Which do you agree with, or are true for you? Give more details.

Example:
I agree that girls grow up more quickly than boys. My younger sister became interested in music two years before I did.

7 What are the best conditions for a child to develop? Complete the 'Helpful' and 'Unhelpful' lists.

Helpful	Unhelpful

> changing schools frequently   eating a lot of fast food   going to bed early
> having a lot of friends   having a lot of money   having supportive parents
> having very strict parents   missing breakfast   mixing with other children
> taking regular exercise   travelling to other countries   watching a lot of TV

8 Rank your 'Helpful' list from the most important to the least important. Discuss your ideas with a partner and give reasons for your choices.

Top of the class

Flavia Bujor

She looks and sounds like any other French teenager as she sits with her fruit juice in a Parisian café, but there is a difference. After moving to Paris from Romania when she was three, Flavia **grew up** reading the stories of *Lord of the Rings* writer JRR Tolkien.

When she was 12, she sat down and wrote a fantasy novel called *The Prophecy of the Stones*. It has sold more than 50,000 copies, is now available in 21 countries and has made her a rich, young woman.

Has success changed her? No. Her parents do not treat her any differently. She still goes to school, does her homework and loves **hanging out** with her friends.

Keira Knightley

When Keira was a young child, her parents were both actors. They had agents who managed their careers. Keira, who **takes after** her parents, wanted to be an actor, too. When she was three, she asked her parents for an agent. Naturally, they refused, but when she was six, Keira was still asking. Finally, they agreed. But they made Keira promise that she would only do acting work in the school holidays.

At the age of 12, Keira made her Hollywood debut in *Star Wars: The Phantom Menace*. But she kept her promise; she finished her school studies before **going into** acting full-time when she was 17. Her fame hasn't changed her home life but it has made her a lot of money.

Marla Olmstead

Just before her second birthday, Marla was at home with her father. He was **looking after** her while trying to paint a picture of his wife. He gave his daughter some paints and left her to play.

Later, he saw her picture and realised that Marla had a special talent. These days, Marla (now five) doesn't feel special; she just enjoys painting. She has already sold about 25 paintings, raising $40,000. Her paintings attract buyers from all around the world.

With such an amazing gift, what does Marla have to say? 'I really, really like piggies.'* 'Me too!' says her three-year-old brother Zane. 'And making paintings,' she adds. 'Me too!' agrees Zane.

Glossary
* piggies = pigs

LANGUAGE STUDY

Likes and dislikes, agreeing and disagreeing

1   Look at these dialogues. In which one is B agreeing? In which one is B disagreeing?

1   A: *I enjoy painting.*   B: *Really? I don't. I prefer cooking.*
2   A: *I can't stand fantasy novels.*   B: *Me neither.*

2   Complete the table. Write *agree* and *disagree*.

Speaker A (makes a statement)			Speaker B (responds to a statement)				
			1 _____	2 _____			
I	really	like enjoy love hate	Me too.	Really? Do you?	I don't.	I prefer	tennis. listen**ing** to music.
		football. watch**ing** TV.					
		don't mind don't like can't stand	Me neither.	Really?	I do. I like it.		

3   Look at the table in Ex 2 and answer these questions.

1   After *I like / enjoy / love / hate*, what form is the verb?
2   How do you agree with *I like / enjoy / love / hate football*?
3   How do you agree with *I don't mind / don't like / can't stand*?
4   After *I prefer*, what form is the verb?

4   Put these words into three lists with these headings: Positive, Negative and Neutral.

can't stand	don't like	don't mind	enjoy	hate	like	love	really don't like	really like

Grammar reference page 26

5   Complete these sentences with the correct form of the verbs.

1   I really enjoy (go) _____ to the coast.
2   I like films, but I prefer (read) _____.
3   I can't stand (listen) _____ to classical music.
4   I don't mind (watch) _____ action movies, but I prefer horror films.
5   I hate (study) _____ but I like (learn) _____.
6   I really like (play) _____ any ball games.

6   Look at the sentences in Ex 5 again. Tick (✓) the statements you agree with, and cross (✗) the statements you disagree with.

7   Work with a partner. Read out the statements in Ex 5 and agree or disagree. Say what you prefer doing, where necessary.

Example: **A:** *I really enjoy going to the coast.*   **B:** *Me too.*

Vocabulary   **1**   Put these words into four lists with these headings: Sports, Leisure activities, Types of film and Styles of music. Add two more of your own to each group.

basketball   comedy   hanging out with friends   hip-hop   horror   karate rap   reading   reggae   science fiction   tennis   watching TV

2   Work with a partner. Say which activities in Ex 1 you like / don't like. In each case, agree or disagree.

Speed-dating

Listening

1 Look at the picture. What is speed-dating?

2 🔘 **02** Listen to three people at a speed-dating evening. Write their names in the table in the order you hear them. Which two people do you think could have a second date?

	Names		
	1 _____	2 _____	3 _____
Reggae music			
Hip-hop music			
Hanging out with friends			
Science-fiction films			
Comedies			
Horror films			
Reading			
Watching TV			

3 Listen again. Complete the table in Ex 2 with a tick (✓) and a cross (✗) for the things each person likes and doesn't like.

4 Work with a partner and discuss these questions.
1 Would you ever go to a speed-dating evening? Why? / Why not?
2 How much do you think someone can find out about you in three minutes?
3 Do you think it's necessary to have the same interests as someone in order to be attracted to them?

Speaking

1 Complete these questions to make nine different questions that *you* would like to answer at a speed-dating evening.
1 What kind of _____ do you like?
2 What kind of _____ do you like?
3 What kind of _____ do you like?
4 Who's your favourite _____?
5 How many _____ have you got?
6 How often do you _____?
7 Where do you _____?
8 Why are you _____?
9 Have you ever _____?

> What kind of films do you like?

2 Work with a partner. Give your questions to your partner and take your partner's questions. Ask and answer your questions. Give details with your answers.

3 When you have finished, find a new partner and repeat Ex 2. Who had the most interesting question, and the most interesting answer?

 **CD-ROM** For more activities go to **Vision Unit 1**

2 Innovation

LEARNING AIMS

- Can talk about past events
- Can make phrases using *make* and *do*
- Can discuss the importance of inventions

▲ Confucius

Great minds

Lead-in

1 Who is the greatest of all time for each category? Discuss your choices in groups.

1 sports personality 2 musician 3 politician 4 scientist

▲ Marie Curie

2 Which of these qualities are necessary to become a great person? Rank them in order of importance. Discuss your ideas with a partner.

a get good results at school / university.
b start young
c believe you can make a difference
d have a lot of money
e think differently from the rest
f have gifted parents

Example:
A: *I think the most important thing is to have a lot of money.*
B: *Really? Why's that?*
A: *Well, it's much easier to achieve great things if you're rich.*
B: *Yes, but …*

▲ Nelson Mandela

Listening

1 🔘 03 Listen to an interview about Steve Jobs, co-founder of Apple. Which qualities in Lead-in Ex 2 are mentioned?

2 Are these statements true or false? Listen again and check your answers.

1 Steve Jobs invented the personal computer with Steve Wozniak.
2 When they met Steve Jobs was 30 and Steve Wozniak was 18.
3 They both wanted to change the world.
4 Steve Wozniak chose the name Apple.
5 Steve Jobs was pushed out of Apple.
6 Steve Jobs never returned to Apple.
7 Steve Jobs changed the colour of computers.

3 Which of the events in the box refer to:

1 Steve Jobs? 2 Apple? 3 Steve Jobs and Steve Wozniak?

a introduced the iPod _2_
b invented the personal computer ___
c met Steve Wozniak ___
d produced brightly-coloured computers ___
e returned to Apple ___
f started Pixar ___
g was pushed out ___
h was valued at $100 million ___

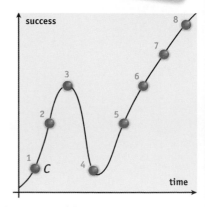

▲ Steve Jobs (left) and Steve Wozniak (right) in 1984.

4 Write the letters a–h from Ex 3 in the correct place on the graph of Steve Jobs' life.

5 Work with a partner. Use the graph in Ex 4 to help you re-tell the story of Steve Jobs.

LANGUAGE STUDY

Talking about past events

Past simple and past continuous

1   Look at this sentence from the interview and answer the questions.

*They **met** for the first time when they **were working** at the same company.*

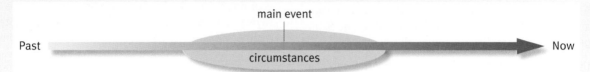

main event

Past

circumstances

Now

1   Which tense is used to talk about the **main event**?
2   Which tense is used to talk about the **circumstances**?
3   In the sentence, which action started first?

Grammar reference page 26

2   Complete these two sentences from the interview with the correct form of the verbs. Think about what the main event was and what the circumstances were.

1   Steve (have) _____ the idea for a home computer when he (pick) _____ apples.

2   Steve (make) _____ the movie Toy Story with his new company, Pixar, when Apple (ask) _____ him to come back.

3   🔘 **04** Listen to these five situations and write a sentence to describe each one. Use the verbs and nouns in the boxes to help you.

Verbs			Nouns		
break down	brush	drive	alarm clock	car	~~doorbell~~
~~have lunch~~	ring	sleep	mobile	teeth	road
start to rain	walk				

Example: *1 He was having lunch when the doorbell rang.*

Regular past tense endings (*-ed*)

Pronunciation   1   🔘 **05** How do these verbs from the interview sound when they are used in the past simple? Complete the table. Then listen and check your answers.

~~ask~~   ~~change~~   ~~decide~~   discover   invent   look   push   return   start

/d/	/t/	/ɪd/
changed	*asked*	*decided*

2   🔘 **06** Practise saying the past simple of these verbs. Listen and check. Then add them to the table in Ex 1.

depart   live   love   want   watch   work

3   Choose one verb from each column of the table in Ex 1 and write three sentences about yourself. Make two sentences true and one sentence false. Read them to a partner and see if he / she can guess which is the false sentence.

Example:

A: *Yesterday I changed my mobile phone number.*
    Earlier today I asked Danni to lend me her DVD player.
    I started golf lessons last weekend.

B: *Golf? But you hate sport!*

Reading 1 🔊 07 Read the report quickly. Which of the toys in the photos is not mentioned?

TOKYO GIZMO

A machine that can translate what your cat is saying and another to control your dreams are just two of the gadgets from Japan's most **innovative** toy maker.

Until recently, Takara was the number two toymaker in Japan. It was making toys like Japanese Barbie and Transformers robots when suddenly everything changed.

It now **produces** a banana-shaped mobile phone, a talking globe and an alarm clock that drops from the ceiling to wake you up. Takara's toys went from boring to bananas! And that was just the beginning.

The change for Takara began when the company's original president came out of **retirement** to save the company. It wasn't making money under the management of the new president, his son.

The new **policy** was fun, fun, fun. New toys were chosen only if they made people laugh. Takara started to do well and sales increased immediately.

One popular toy is the Bowlingual dog translator. When your dog barks, the Bowlingual tells you what he is saying. 'I'm happy,' or 'I need love,' are two favourites. Another new toy is the Meowlingual, which does the same as the Bowlingual, but this time for cats.

Takara also sells full-sized versions of its toy cars – some people even go to work in theirs! But Takara's next invention was even more unusual – a machine that can control your dreams. You feed the gadget a picture connected to the dream you want to have, choose a **scent** and soft music, then start it. During the night it plays the music and releases the scent. But it doesn't always work out as expected. One tester wanted to dream that he was playing football for Japan in the World Cup. Instead he dreamed that he was watching the game on TV with just a packet of crisps for company!

Based on an article from Night and Day magazine.

▲ full-sized toy car

▼ dream machine

2 Read the text again and answer these questions.
1 What toys were the company making before the big change?
2 What was unusual about the company's:
   a mobile phone?
   b globe?
   c alarm clock?
3 Why did the ex-president come out of retirement?
4 What does the Meowlingual do?
5 Can you drive the toy cars on the road?
6 What did one dream machine tester hope for?
7 What did he actually dream?

3 What gizmos have you seen recently that are:
   a fun?
   b a bit silly?

▲ cat translator

▲ talking globe

▲ aquaroid jellyfish robot

4 Find these words in the text and complete the sentences.

| innovative | produces | retirement | policy | scent |

1 France definitely _____ the best wine in the world.
2 I love the _____ of *Chanel No 5*.
3 The music industry isn't _____ any more. They don't have any new ideas.
4 The perfect age for _____ is 50. You can still enjoy yourself then.
5 I'm not really interested in the government's _____ on education in my country.

5 Change four of the sentences in Ex 4 to express your own opinions. Compare your sentences with a partner.

Example: *I love the scent of fresh flowers.*

make and *do*

Vocabulary **1** Look at these examples of *make* and *do* from the text. Complete the lists using the words and phrases in the box.

*New toys were chosen only if they **made people laugh**.*
*Takara started to **do well** and sales increased immediately.*

Make	*Do*
someone laugh / cry	well / badly

| a decision an exam a mistake a phone call business money some damage someone angry someone a favour ~~someone laugh / cry~~ ~~well / badly~~ your homework |

2 Complete these questions with the correct form of *make* or *do*.

1 Do you like _____*doing*_____ homework?
2 What _____ you laugh?
3 When was the last time you _____ an international phone call?
4 Have you ever _____ really badly in an exam?
5 How much money do you want to _____ in the next ten years?
6 Have you ever _____ some damage and then not admitted it?

3 Work with a partner. Ask and answer the questions in Ex 2.

Most important for the world

Speaking **1** 🔘 **08** You are going to play a team game. Listen to the example. Which argument do you think is stronger?

2 Work in three groups: Group 1, 2 and 3. Read how to play, then play the game.

How to play

1 Each member of the group chooses a number between 1 and 6. Don't choose the same number.
2 Turn to page 29 to find the object you have chosen.
3 You are going to argue against a member of another group. You have to say why your object is more important for the world than your opponent's.
4 You have five minutes to prepare what you are going to say.
5 During each match, one group will be the jury and decide which player from the other two groups gave the best argument.

CD-ROM For more activities go to **Vision Unit 2**

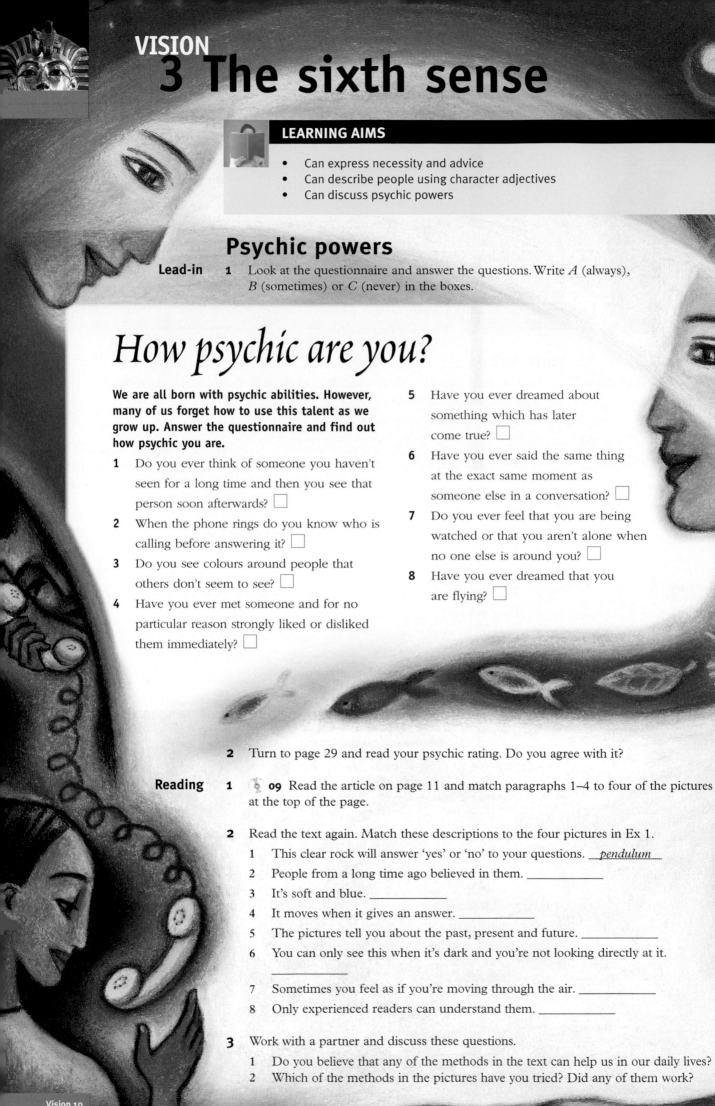

3 The sixth sense

LEARNING AIMS

- Can express necessity and advice
- Can describe people using character adjectives
- Can discuss psychic powers

Psychic powers

Lead-in **1** Look at the questionnaire and answer the questions. Write *A* (always), *B* (sometimes) or *C* (never) in the boxes.

How psychic are you?

We are all born with psychic abilities. However, many of us forget how to use this talent as we grow up. Answer the questionnaire and find out how psychic you are.

1 Do you ever think of someone you haven't seen for a long time and then you see that person soon afterwards? ☐

2 When the phone rings do you know who is calling before answering it? ☐

3 Do you see colours around people that others don't seem to see? ☐

4 Have you ever met someone and for no particular reason strongly liked or disliked them immediately? ☐

5 Have you ever dreamed about something which has later come true? ☐

6 Have you ever said the same thing at the exact same moment as someone else in a conversation? ☐

7 Do you ever feel that you are being watched or that you aren't alone when no one else is around you? ☐

8 Have you ever dreamed that you are flying? ☐

2 Turn to page 29 and read your psychic rating. Do you agree with it?

Reading **1** 09 Read the article on page 11 and match paragraphs 1–4 to four of the pictures at the top of the page.

2 Read the text again. Match these descriptions to the four pictures in Ex 1.

1 This clear rock will answer 'yes' or 'no' to your questions. *pendulum*

2 People from a long time ago believed in them. _____

3 It's soft and blue. _____

4 It moves when it gives an answer. _____

5 The pictures tell you about the past, present and future. _____

6 You can only see this when it's dark and you're not looking directly at it. _____

7 Sometimes you feel as if you're moving through the air. _____

8 Only experienced readers can understand them. _____

3 Work with a partner and discuss these questions.

1 Do you believe that any of the methods in the text can help us in our daily lives?

2 Which of the methods in the pictures have you tried? Did any of them work?

horoscopes

I-ching

tarot cards

tea leaves

palm reading

aura

dreams

crystal ball

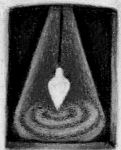
pendulum

Develop your powers

So, we all have psychic powers? How can we develop them? A new book by psychic Rolando Jamel offers his advice. He says that you don't have to be an expert – everyone can increase their psychic powers. All it takes is practice.

1   It's a crystal on the end of a string. You use it to answer questions. Hold the string between the thumb and forefinger. You must think about nothing else – clear your mind. Ask it to show you the answer 'yes'. It will begin swinging gently from side to side and then in a circular motion. Then ask it to show 'no'. It will circle in the opposite direction. You can even use it to choose the best place for your next holiday by asking it questions with yes or no answers.

2   It's a field of energy around every living thing. Some people can see a soft, blue light around people. Try it yourself. To see it around your hand more clearly, you should turn the lights down and relax. Put out one hand, palm downwards and look beyond the hand. Soon a fine outline of electric blue light around your fingers will begin to appear.

3   They're picture cards with special symbols and meanings. There are many different ways to lay them out. The simplest is to place seven in a row, face down. Turn over the cards one at a time. The first two cards show the recent past, the middle three, the present, and the final two, the future. You have to know the meaning of each card before you can understand their message. People usually visit special readers who are able to interpret the meaning of the cards.

4   We all do it, but do they tell us about the future? Ancient civilisations believed they did, and there are many today who still believe it. And if, in your sleep, you feel you're flying, then this is called an 'out-of-body experience'. It happens to about 35% of people. To remember your dreams, you should write them down as soon as you wake up in the morning.

LANGUAGE STUDY

Expressing necessity and advice

1 Look at the words in **bold** in these sentences and answer the questions.

*He says that you **don't have to** be an expert.   You **must** think about nothing else but the pendulum.*
*To see the aura more clearly, you **should** turn the lights down and relax.*

Which means: 1 'it's necessary'?   2 'it's a good idea'?   3 'it's not necessary'?

2 Which verb form follows the words in **bold** in Ex 1?

3 Match *ought to*, *have to* and *don't have to* to the definitions in Ex 1.

4 Complete the table using the words and phrases in Ex 1 and 3.

It's necessary to do it	It's not necessary to do it (but you can if you want to)	It's a good idea to do it
_____ _____	_____ _____	_____
It's necessary not to do it *mustn't* _____		**It's not a good idea to do it** *shouldn't* _____

Grammar reference page 27

5 Complete these sentences using words and phrases from the table in Ex 4. Use the words in brackets to help you.

1 You *must / have to* try harder. It's the only way you'll improve. (necessary)

2 The manager _____ change some of the players in the team. (a good idea)

3 You _____ if you don't want to. It's your choice. (not necessary)

4 I know I _____ bite my fingernails, but I can't help it. (not a good idea)

5 You _____ do anything that will upset her. (necessary not to)

6 Turn to page 32 and complete the 'Find someone who ...' activity.

Writing

1 Marco is going to visit his friend, Mahmoud, in Saudi Arabia. He has written to him asking these questions. Read Mahmoud's email and find the answers.

1 Should I bring a lot of clothes – what's the weather like at this time of year?
2 Do I have to wear special clothes?
3 Can I visit a religious building?
4 Is there anything you can think of that I should / shouldn't do in your country?

2 Imagine that Marco is going to visit you in your country. Write an email reply to him. Use the questions in Ex 1 and Mahmoud's email to help you.

I'm really pleased that you're coming to Saudi Arabia. I'll show you the markets (souks) and the Khuzam Palace Gardens.

To answer your questions: you don't need to bring a lot of clothes – it's warm here, even in winter. You asked if you can visit a religious building. Yes, I'll take you to Ma'mar Masjid Mosque. You don't have to wear special clothes, but you must cover your legs (don't wear shorts) and your arms as a mark of respect. It's such a beautiful building, I'm sure you'll really like it, but you mustn't photograph it.

What else can I tell you? When someone offers you tea or coffee, you shouldn't refuse. And you ought to try to learn one or two words of Arabic. Don't worry, though, I'll be with you and you'll be fine. I'm looking forward to seeing you.

Mahmoud

Character adjectives

Vocabulary and speaking

1 Look at the pictures and complete these definitions.

1 A ___sensitive___ person cares about other people, and feels emotions strongly.
2 A _____ person is always ready to do something to help you.
3 A _____ person doesn't talk very much.
4 A _____ person needs a lot of attention and is not easily pleased.
5 A _____ person thinks only about himself / herself and not others.
6 A _____ person believes in his / her own ability.
7 A _____ person is reasonable and practical, and doesn't take risks.
8 A _____ person is pleasant and kind towards other people.
9 An _____ person easily becomes upset by things people do or say to them.
10 A _____ person doesn't trust other people.
11 A _____ person is nervous and embarrassed when meeting new people.
12 A _____ person is not at all interesting.

2 Work with a partner. Describe three people you know using the adjectives in Ex 1. Give as much detail as possible.

Example:
My friend Mark's a really friendly person. He's always very helpful to other people, and he's very sensitive when I want to share a problem with him.

Your lying ways

Listening

1 Work with a partner. Look at these pictures of sleeping people and discuss the questions.

1 Which position do you sleep in?
2 Do you think our sleeping position tells us something about our character?

2 🔘 **10** Listen to a radio report about sleeping styles. As you listen, write two adjectives from Vocabulary and speaking Ex 1 under each picture.

3 Answer these questions. Listen again and check your answers.

1 What is the most popular sleeping position?
2 What percentage of people sleep in this position?
3 In which sleeping position do you look like a tree that's fallen down?
4 Which categories of sleeper make good friends?
5 In which sleeping positions will you probably snore?

4 Do the adjectives for your sleeping position describe you? If not, which adjectives do?

Foetus
_____

Log
_____

Yearner
_____

Soldier
_____

Freefaller
_____

Starfish
_____

CD-ROM For more activities go to **Vision Unit 3**

4 What do you do?

LEARNING AIMS

- Can make promises, requests and predictions
- Can talk about jobs and career choices
- Can understand texts about work experiences

Any volunteers?

Lead-in **1** These people have all decided to take time out after graduating from university. Read what they say and answer the questions.

> I want to travel around picking fruit.

> I'd like to work as an au pair.

> I plan to teach in another country as a volunteer.

> I'm going to be a children's camp activity leader.

1 Which job would you enjoy doing the most?
2 In which country?   3 For how long?

Reading **1** **11** Novelist Justin Hill worked in another country after graduating from university. Read his story and compare your answers in Lead-in Ex 1 to what Justin did. Are any of your answers the same?

Life
as I now know it

When I told my mother what I had decided to do after graduating from university, she cried. Friends told me that I was **crazy**. 'What are you going to do for money?' they demanded. One even said that I should grow up and become responsible. I was surprised by their reaction. After all, I had only decided to go **abroad** and work with Voluntary Service Overseas (VSO). Surely, this was a good thing to do – wasn't it?

Every year the VSO sends 2,000 people of all ages to different countries, where they spend two years working. They are paid the same money as a local person doing the same job. They have a wide range of **skills**: nurses, teachers, engineers, plumbers, architects, computer programmers and agricultural workers.

A week after my interview I received a letter offering me a place in China. I went on one or two courses before going. We talked about the challenges that we would face: loneliness and homesickness. And then, soon afterwards, I and 40 other volunteers left for Beijing.

The **aim** of the Chinese VSO programme was to improve English teaching throughout the country, especially in rural areas. I was sent to a small town called Yuncheng, with a population of about 100,000, and started working in an English department run by Dean Niu. He was a **charming** man who regularly invited us round for parties.

On my first day at work, my students were silent. I was the first Westerner that they had ever seen. But as time passed and friendships **developed**, I realised how much I was learning myself. I learnt the language and began to understand the culture and the people around me. I realised that cultural differences are **superficial**. We are all far more similar than we are different.

When I left China after two and a half years, I had enjoyed the experience so much that I decided to go again.

The Drink and Dream Teahouse
Justin Hill

2 Read the text again and answer these questions.

1 What did Justin's friends think about his decision to become a volunteer?
2 How long does a normal contract with VSO last?
3 What did Justin think of the man who ran the English department?
4 What did he learn about people from different cultures?

3 Find these words in the text. Match them to their definitions.

aim abbroad charming crazy developed skills superficial

1 ability to do things well = _____
2 not sensible or practical = _____
3 attractive and pleasant = _____
4 in or to a foreign country = _____
5 not very strong or important = _____
6 something you hope to achieve = _____
7 grown or changed = _____

4 Complete these sentences using the words in Ex 3.

1 I try to go _____ at least once a year.
2 It's better to have a wide range of _____ rather than be very good at just one thing.
3 My _____ in life is to get a job in which I can help others.
4 I only have a _____ interest in sports – I watch them sometimes but I never do them.
5 I think it's _____ to refuse a well-paid job. Even if it is boring, think of the money!
6 It's more important to be _____ than clever.
7 My best friendships have _____ over many years. They didn't happen overnight.

5 Which sentences in Ex 4 are true for you or do you agree with? Discuss your ideas with a partner.

Occupations

Vocabulary **1** Justin said that the occupations in the box were popular in VSO. Which would be good for someone who likes:

1 creating things? 3 working with tools?
2 helping people? 4 solving problems?

agricultural worker architect computer programmer engineer nurse plumber teacher

2 How many more occupations can you think of for each of the categories in Ex 1?

3 What is your ideal occupation? Why?

4 According to psychologist John Holland, the occupation you choose to do depends on your personality. To discover your ideal occupation, turn to page 29 and take the test.

Listening

1 Kelly Hunter replied to this advertisement and has been accepted by the organisation. Read the advertisement and answer these questions.

1 Where is she going?
2 For how long?
3 What does she have to do there?
4 How much does she have to pay for her food and travel?

2 🔘 **12** Kelly is getting ready to leave in four days. Listen to her conversation with her mother. Tick (✓) the things Kelly's mother mentions.

accidents ☐   food ☐

illness ☐   transport ☐

animals ☐   romance ☐

3 Would you do what Kelly is going to do? Do you think her mother is right to be worried? Discuss your ideas in groups.

VOLUNTEERS NEEDED

Help the Children

needs young people in Papua New Guinea for 8-week aid programme.

Your duties: to help local health workers to distribute medical supplies.

All flights, accommodation and meals are provided as part of the contract.

Up-to-date passport essential.

All enquiries to Stefan Baros at:
21 Hanover
London W
Or em

LANGUAGE STUDY

Making promises, requests and predictions: *will*

1 Look at these sentences from Kelly's conversation with her mother. Which sentence is:

1 a promise / offer? ☐   a *I'll have a cup of tea, please.*

2 a request / order? ☐   b *I'll be OK – I'll be fine, really.*

3 a prediction? ☐   c *I'll call you every week, honestly.*

2 Look at these sentences and the sentences in Ex 1. Are statements 1–3 true (✓) or false (✗)?

Mum: *Will they feed you properly?*   **Mum:** *You might get malaria.*
Kelly: *I'm sure they will.*   **Kelly:** *I won't. I'm taking anti-malaria tablets.*

1 If *will* appears within a positive statement, but not at the end of it, it is often contracted to *'ll.* ☐

2 *Will* is never contracted (*'ll*) in questions or short answers. ☐

3 The negative of *will* is *won't.* ☐

Grammar reference page 27

3 Look at these sentences and decide which is:
a a promise / offer.   b a request / order.   c a prediction.

1 I'll cut taxes and I'll introduce free health care. You have my word on that.

2 OK, everybody. Will you sit in a circle, please?

3 It'll probably take about two hours to fix this pipe.

4 Will you open just a little wider, please?

5 Your heart's fine – you'll live longer than all of us.

6 Fuel problem? Sure. I'll take a look right now.

4 🔘 **13** Look at the sentences in Ex 3 again. What occupation do you think each person has? Listen and check your ideas.

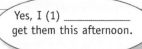

Yes, I (1) _____ get them this afternoon.

Yes. Yes, I (2) _____. All right … But … but … (3) _____ you?

OK, thanks. No, I (4) _____. I never do. Don't worry … OK, OK, I (5) _____ see you later.

5 14 Complete this telephone conversation using *will*, *'ll* or *won't*. Listen and check your answers.

6 Who do you think this conversation is between and what are they talking about?

7 Look at these sentences. Who's talking each time? Who are they talking to? Where are they? Discuss your ideas with a partner.

1 I think I'll have the fish, please.
2 Jane, will you promise to love John for as long as you both live?
3 I'll call you back, darling. I'm in a meeting right now.
4 Will someone get the phone? I'm chopping onions!
5 The line's busy – will you hold?
6 One coat and one jacket. It won't take long. It'll be ready at 4.00.

Speaking

1 Read this dialogue between Nathan and his friend, Saira. Underline examples of:

a a promise / offer   b a request / order   c a prediction.

Situation: You've decided to take flying lessons
Nathan: I've decided to take flying lessons.
Saira: You're crazy. It's very dangerous. Will you be OK?
Nathan: Sure. I'll be fine.
Saira: How many lessons do you have to take before you can fly alone?
Nathan: About fifteen. I'll take you up if you like.
Saira: No, thank you. I only fly when I absolutely have to.
Nathan: OK, but will you come and watch?
Saira: What do you mean?
Nathan: When I go up on my own for the first time – will you come?
Saira: Oh, sure. Just so long as I can stay on the ground.

2 Work with a partner. Choose one of these situations and write a short dialogue between you and one of your friends, using Ex 1 to help you. Include at least one promise / offer, one request / order and one prediction.

Situations:
1 You're going to climb Mount Everest with your climbing club.
2 You've decided to buy a motorbike.
3 You've arranged a scuba diving holiday.
4 You've arranged to do volunteer work in a country at war.

3 Practise your dialogue. Then act it out to another pair. They have to find your uses of *will* (promise / offer, request / order and prediction).

Find my job

4 Work in groups. Read how to play 'Find my job', then play the game.

How to play
Think of a job, but don't tell anyone. Each person in the group asks you a question. You can only answer 'yes' or 'no'. If the other players haven't guessed your job after asking ten questions, you get five points. If they guess your job, they each get two points. The player with the most points at the end wins.

Do you … build things? help people? use a computer?
Do you work … inside? outside? in an office?

CD-ROM For more activities go to **Vision Unit 4**

5 Review

Lead-in **1** Work in groups and discuss these questions.

1 What do you like about your job / studies? What don't you like?
2 Do you know anybody who left their job / studies and did something completely different? What did they do?

Language study

1 🔘 **15** Thomas Hunter recently gave up his job to sail around the world. Listen to the interview. How long does Thomas think he'll be away?

2 Listen again and choose the correct alternative.

1 Thomas gave up his job because he:
    a didn't like his place of work. b didn't earn much money.
    c didn't like the other people in his office.

2 When he was looking on the internet, he found:
    a an advert for a water sports holiday. b a good sailing club near his house.
    c a cheap boat.

3 He decided to leave his job:
    a after a few sailing lessons. b during his first sailing lesson.
    c before he began sailing lessons.

4 Which word best describes Thomas?
    a shy b confident c demanding

5 Thomas thinks other people:
    a should never leave their jobs. b should travel around the world.
    c should do things they enjoy.

6 Thomas promises he will:
    a come back for another interview. b send emails to the interviewer.
    c phone from every country.

3 Complete these sentences from the interview with the correct form of the verbs. Look at listening script 15 on page 31 to check your answers.

1 The truth is that I can't stand (be) _____ indoors all the time.
2 I like (do) _____ sport and other outdoor activities.
3 I (look) _____ on the internet when I saw an advert for a boat.
4 I (sail) _____ across the lake when I had the idea.
5 I (go) _____ into work the next day and told my manager.
6 Do you think you have to (be) _____ a good sailor to travel so far?
7 I don't need to (earn) _____ any money for a while.
8 I like (be) _____ on my own.
9 They should (not do) _____ things they (not want) _____ to do.
10 (you / come) _____ and see us when you get back?

4 Work in groups. What do you like doing in your free time? Discuss the ideas in the box.

cooking listening to music painting playing ball games reading studying watching films watching TV

Example:
A: *I love listening to music.*
B: *Me too. I like reggae.*
C: *Really? I don't mind reggae, but I prefer rap.*

Vocabulary

KEY

 Name a style of music.

 Name a type of film.

 Name a sport.

 Name a leisure activity.

 Name an occupation.

 Describe someone using a character adjective.

 Make a sentence with *make* or *do*.

1 Work in a group of two to four players. Read how to play the 'Life steps' game, then play the game.

How to play

1. Each player needs a counter and each group needs a dice.
2. Take it in turns to throw the dice and move your counter.
3. Look at the colour of the square and the key. You have 30 seconds to think of a word in this word group.
4. If the word is correct, you stay on your square. If the word is wrong or you can't think of a word, you move back to your original square. You must not repeat a word already used.
5. When you land on a Life step, follow the instructions and the next player takes his / her turn.
6. The first player to reach the finish is the winner.

Song

1 Read the factfile about Nelly Furtado and answer these questions.

1 How did Nelly first become interested in singing?
2 What instrument influenced her earlier music?
3 How many languages does she sing in?
4 When did she release her first album?

factfile

Nelly Furtado was born on 2 December, 1978 and grew up in Victoria, Canada. She got her first tape recorder when she was eight and used it to record herself singing. When she was 14, she enjoyed listening to music produced with a drum machine. You can hear that interest in her first album.

Nelly Furtado has a really original and interesting music style. Her music is a mixture of hip-hop, funk, world music and jazz. She's also very talented. She sings in English, Portuguese and Hindi and can play the guitar, the ukulele and the trombone.

Nelly first became successful at a talent show in Toronto when the manager of another big band noticed her ability. Soon afterwards, she signed a record deal with DreamWorks and released her first album *Whoa! Nelly* in September 2000. The first single *I'm like a bird* flew up the charts.

2 🔘 **16** Listen to the song. Who do you think the woman is singing about?

I'm like a bird

You're beautiful, that's for sure
You'll never ever fade
You're lovely but it's not for sure
That I won't ever change
And though my love is rare
Though my love is true

Chorus

I'm like a bird, I'll only fly away
I don't know where my soul is,
I don't know where my home is
(and baby all I need for you to know is)
I'm like a bird, I'll only fly away
I don't know where my soul is,
I don't know where my home is
All I need for you to know is

Your faith in me brings me to tears
Even after all these years
And it pains me so much to tell
That you don't know me that well
And though my love is rare
Though my love is true

Chorus

It's not that I wanna say goodbye
It's just that every time you try to
tell me that you love me
Each and every single day I know
I'm going to have to eventually
give you away
And though my love is rare
And though my love is true
Hey I'm just scared
That we may fall through

Chorus

3 Answer these questions.

Verse 1: 1 How does the singer describe the man?
2 Does she think she'll love him forever?
Verse 2: 3 What doesn't she like about the man?
4 How does she describe her love for him?
Verse 3: 5 Why doesn't she want him to say he loves her?
6 How does she feel about the relationship?

4 Which statement do you think best describes the singer's feelings?

1 She loves the man and really wants to stay with him forever.
2 She loves the man, but she doesn't think they have a future.
3 She doesn't love the man and wants to find somebody else.

5 Discuss these questions.

1 Why do you think the singer describes herself as a bird?
2 What do you think the singer will do? What do you think the singer should do?
3 Do you think it's possible to love someone but not want to be with them? Why? Have you ever felt like this?

Speaking: a TV advice show

1 Work in groups of four. You are going to take part in a TV advice show called *Life story*. Follow the instructions.

Step 1: **Prepare the information you need**
- In your group, each choose a character:
  - a guest with a problem
  - a friend or relative of the guest
  - a presenter for the show
  - a psychologist
- Plan the answers to the questions on your role card.

Step 2: **Practise your show**
It should last five or ten minutes.

Step 3: **Perform your show**
When each group performs, the audience should clap, cheer or boo as appropriate. The audience can also offer their opinion and give advice to the guest.

Life story
THE GUEST

- What's your name?
- How old are you?
- What do you do? (e.g. architect / student / unemployed)
- Where do you live? (e.g. with parents / alone / with friends / no permanent address)
- Do you have a relationship? (e.g. married / single / serious boyfriend / girlfriend.
- What's your problem? (e.g. can't settle down in a job / a relationship; spend too much money on travel / shopping; hang out with the wrong people)

Life story
THE PRESENTER

- What's your name?
- How will you introduce the show and the guest? (e.g. *Welcome to 'Life Story'. On today's programme, we have a very interesting guest. His / Her name is … and He's / She's …*)
- What questions will you ask the guest?
- When will you introduce the psychologist and the friend / relative?
- When will you ask the audience for their opinion / advice?
- What opinion / advice will you give to the guest? (e.g. *I agree with …, I think you should …*)
- How will you close the show? (e.g. *And that's all we've got time for …*)

Life story
THE FRIEND OR RELATIVE

- What's your name?
- What relationship do you have with the guest? (e.g. boyfriend / girlfriend / flatmate / parent)
- Why does the guest's problem worry you?
- How would you describe the guest? (e.g. selfish, demanding, over sensitive)
- What opinion / advice will you give the guest? (e.g. *You must / mustn't …, You should / shouldn't …*)

Life story
THE PSYCHOLOGIST

- What's your name?
- Why do you think the guest has this problem?
- What opinion / advice will you give the guest? (e.g. *You must / mustn't …, You should / shouldn't …*)

VISION
Extra practice

Unit 1

1 Choose the correct alternative.

1   I grew *up / on / in* listening to a lot of music.

2   My parents both worked when I was a child, so my grandmother often looked *at / with / after* me.

3   I usually hang *into / out / for* with my friends at the weekend.

4   I think I take *off / away / after* my uncle because we both loving painting.

5   I'd like to go *into / for / by* the music industry.

2 Complete the dialogue with the words in the box.

> too   stand   really   you   neither
> studying   hate   prefer

Ben: I started a new film studies class last night.

Mena: (1) _____? I don't like

(2) _____ in the evening.

Ben: Me (3) _____, but I've got a job now.

Mena: Me (4) _____. I work at the college. Where do you work?

Ben: At the cinema. I get cheap tickets. Do you want some?

Mena: Fantastic. What's on?

Ben: There's a new science fiction film.

Mena: Oh. Actually, I can't (5) _____ watching films about space.

Ben: Well … Do you like romantic comedies?

Mena: No! I (6) _____ romantic comedies! I (7) _____ horror.

Ben: Do (8) _____? How about *The Night of the Dead*? It's on tonight.

Mena: Fantastic! Thanks, Ben. See you later!

3 Complete these opinions. Then write your own replies.

Example:

A: I like (play) _*playing*_ basketball.

B: _I don't. I prefer football._

1   A: I love (watch) _____ action movies.

B: _____

2   A: I hate (listen) _____ to classical music.

B: _____

3   A: I don't mind (read) _____ fantasy novels.

B: _____

4   A: I don't like (eat) _____ in restaurants.

B: _____

4 Complete the crossword.

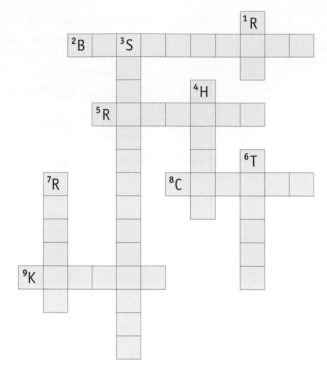

Clues

1   This is a type of music where people speak over a strong beat. (3)

2   You can have a total of five players on the court in your team in this game. (10)

3   This type of film is about imaginary future events and usually involves space travel. (7, 7)

4   This is a type of music that uses rap and samples of music from other songs. (3-3)

5   Words related to this leisure activity are *best-seller, novel, author* and *stories*. (7)

6   Words related to this sport are *racket, ball, court* and *Wimbledon*. (6)

7   This is a type of music that came from Jamaica in the 1960s. (7)

8   This type of film makes people laugh. (6)

9   This is a Japanese martial art. (6)

5 Put these words in the correct order to make questions.

1   music   like?   kind   you   What   do   of

_____

2   is   Who   film star?   your   favourite

_____

3   have   How   you   brothers   got?   many

_____

4   restaurants?   eat   How   you   often   in   do

_____

5   Where   you   hanging out?   like   do

_____

Unit 2

1 Complete the interview with the correct form of the verbs in the box.

> be   not be   become   not earn   get   not go
> give   meet   work

We interviewed Paul Smith, three-time winner of the Young Inventor of the Year.

Q   Why did you (1) _____ an inventor?

A   When I was five, I (2) _____ an inventor friend of my father's. I was really interested in his work.

Q   What was your first invention?

A   A kind of car, but it (3) _____ very good because it (4) _____ very fast!

Q   What about school? Did you (5) _____ good results?

A   Yes, I did. I always (6) _____ hard at school.

Q   Inventing is an expensive business. Did your parents (7) _____ you any money?

A   Yes, they did. I had a part-time job but I (8) _____ enough money so they helped me. They (9) _____ really supportive actually.

Q   So you shared the prize money with them?

A   Um … not really!

2 Choose the correct alternative.

1   I *cycling* / *was cycling* in the park when I *saw* / *was seeing* Theo with his new girlfriend.

2   Luckily, the car *didn't break down* / *wasn't breaking down* when we *drove* / *were driving* on the motorway.

3   They *ate* / *were eating* lunch when they *heard* / *were hearing* the news.

4   I *didn't buy* / *wasn't buying* anything when I *shopped* / *was shopping* this afternoon.

5   It *started* / *was starting* to rain when I *sat* / *was sitting* on the beach.

6   I *didn't listen* / *wasn't listening* when my manager *asked* / *was asking* me a question in the meeting.

7   I *looked* / *was looking* on the internet when I *found* / *was finding* a great website.

8   I *slept* / *was sleeping* when you *called* / *were calling*.

3 Complete the texts with the past simple or past continuous form of the verbs.

There are lots of stories about accidental inventions. Are they myth or are they reality? Read these stories. Do you believe them?

A long time ago, a boy called Frank Epperson (1 drink) _____ a cold drink outside his house when he (2 decide) _____ to go back inside. That night, the weather was very cold. The next morning, when Frank (3 look for) _____ his drink, he (4 discover) _____ the world's first ice lolly!

In 1853, a chef (5 work) _____ in a restaurant when a customer (6 complain) _____ about the potatoes. The customer said they were too big and they (7 not be) _____ cooked. The chef was annoyed, so he cut up the potatoes very thin and cooked them for a very long time. The customer (8 love) _____ these first potato crisps!

A doctor (9 experiment) _____ with a new medicine when two businessmen (10 drink) _____ some of it. The businessmen (11 not think) _____ it was good medicine, but they (12 like) _____ the taste. It became Coca-Cola!

4 Complete these dialogues with the correct form of *make* or *do*.

1   A: How was the exam? Did you _____ well?
    B: No, I _____ a lot of mistakes.

2   A: We would like to _____ business with you.
    B: Great! I'll _____ a phone call to the manager.

3   A: That film was really sad. Did it _____ you cry?
    B: No, it _____ me laugh; it was really stupid.

4   A: Have you ever _____ a really bad decision?
    B: Yes, I didn't _____ a favour for a good friend and it _____ her angry.

5   A: Our shop didn't _____ much money last year.
    B: I know. That new supermarket _____ us a lot of damage.

Unit 3

1 Choose the correct alternative.

Harry: I want to stop smoking.
Kora: You (1) *mustn't / have to* stop! It's really bad for you.
Harry: I know, but what can I do? I've tried everything.
Kora: You (2) *ought to / don't have to* see a hypnotherapist.
Harry: Really? Where can I find one?
Kora: You (3) *should / don't need to* look on the internet, but you (4) *needn't / must* be careful. Not all hypnotherapists are qualified.
Harry: What do I (5) *have to / must* say to the hypnotherapist?
Kora: You (6) *don't need to / mustn't* say very much because he will understand your problem.
Harry: Have you got any other advice?
Kora: Yes. You (7) *must / mustn't* worry. Lots of people have hypnotherapy to stop smoking.

2 Complete these sentences with the words in the box.

> don't have to   don't need   have   must
> mustn't   ought   should   shouldn't

1 I'm not working tomorrow so I _____ get up early.

2 You look really tired. You _____ stay out so late every night.

3 I can't wear my own clothes in this job; I _____ to wear a uniform.

4 We _____ make a noise when we get home from the party. My sister and her baby are staying at our house tonight.

5 If you've got a headache, you _____ to take an aspirin and go back to bed for a while.

6 I think you _____ spend less time with your girlfriend and more time studying; you've got an important exam next week.

7 Thank you for a dinner but I _____ go now. The last train home leaves in ten minutes.

8 You _____ to be good at football to play with us. We just play for fun.

3 Rearrange these letters to find ten character adjectives. The first letter is given each time.

Example:
dlfirney = f*riendly*

1 iosupscisu   s_____
2 fcndionte   c_____
3 hys   s_____
4 bngroi   b_____
5 pfheull   h_____
6 shsflei   s_____
7 iblesnse   s_____
8 dennmgadi   d_____
9 sevitines   s_____
10 eiqut   q_____

4 Match some of the character adjectives in Ex 3 to the things these people say.

1 My brother doesn't trust many people.

2 I think we should leave early so we don't get stuck in traffic.

3 He isn't very interesting; all he talks about is science fiction films.

4 I believe I'm very good at sport.

5 She's always ready to do things for you.

6 He only thinks about himself.

7 My little sister always wants something.

8 It's not that she's shy, she just doesn't say very much.

5 Describe yourself using the character adjectives in Ex 3. Give as much detail as possible.

Example:
I'm friendly because I always talk to people, but sometimes I'm a little shy when I'm in a big group of people that I don't know very well.

_____

_____

_____

_____

Unit 4

1 Match two sentences to each job.

1 nurse ☐ ☐

2 teacher ☐ ☐

3 plumber *a* ☐

4 architect ☐ ☐

5 computer programmer ☐ ☐

6 agricultural worker ☐ ☐

a I have a practical job.

b I draw and design houses.

c I help people when they are sick.

d I solve problems.

e I travel and pick fruit.

f I work in a hospital.

g I work in a school or a college.

h I work outside.

i I work with children or adults.

j I work with computers in an office.

k I work with tools and machines.

l My job is creative.

2 Put these words in the correct order to make promises / offers, requests or predictions.

1 day phone I'll every you

_____

2 sandwich? a Will me you make

_____

3 manager I'll to speak my

_____

4 some Will me coffee? you buy

_____

5 it fantastic! will be think I

_____

6 thanks No, won't It today rain

_____

7 have two please I'll coffees,

_____

8 tell won't I anyone

_____

3 Match the responses in Ex 2 to these situations.

a Your friend is looking for a new job. ☐

b You're at your friend's house and you're hungry. ☐

c Your mother doesn't want you to work abroad. ☐

d You are in a café. ☐

e Your father offers you his umbrella. ☐

f Your friend is going to the supermarket. ☐

g A friend tells you a secret. ☐

h Your sister describes the holidays she's planning. ☐

4 Are the responses in Ex 2 promises, offers, requests or predictions?

1 *promise*

2 _____

3 _____

4 _____

5 _____

6 _____

7 _____

8 _____

5 What do you say in these situations? Write sentences.
Example:
You're at the cinema with a friend. Offer to buy the tickets.
I'll buy the tickets.

1 You're going on holiday. Promise to send your friend a postcard.

_____

2 It's a sunny morning. Predict the weather for the afternoon.

_____

3 You can't do your homework. Ask your English teacher to help you.

_____

4 Your mother can't find her car keys. Offer to help her look.

_____

5 You're in a café. Order a cup of coffee and a cheese sandwich.

_____

Grammar reference

Unit 1

Likes and dislikes

You can use these verbs to talk about things you like or dislike:
love, enjoy, like, don't mind, don't like, can't stand, hate.

They are usually followed by a noun or by the *-ing* form of the verb.
I love dancing.
I can't stand football.

In American English particularly, the infinitive can also be used with some of the verbs (*like, love, hate*).
I like to swim.
I hate to eat broccoli.

Agreeing

You use **too** when you want to agree with a positive statement.
A: *I enjoy swimming.*   **B:** *Me **too**.*

You use **neither** when you want to agree with a negative statement.
A: *I can't stand heavy metal music.*   **B:** *Me **neither**.*

The sense is not necessarily negative.
A: *I don't mind cleaning the house.*   **B:** *Me **neither**.*

Disagreeing

There are many ways to disagree. A common, short response is to express your doubts about the other person's idea (*Really?*) and then add a short answer to disagree, usually *I do / don't*.
A: *I love classical music.*   **B:** *Really? I don't.*
A: *I can't stand romantic films.*   **B:** *Really? I like them.*

Unit 2

Talking about past events

Past simple
Form
Many regular verbs end in *-d* or *-ed*.

hire	→	hired
order	→	ordered

There are many irregular verbs, which have different endings in the past.

break	→	broke
see	→	saw

Past simple endings do not change in the third person, as they do with the present simple. The verb *be* is an exception (*I / He / She / It was, You / We / They were*).

I	
You	
He / She / It	hired
We	broke
They	

Use

You use the past simple to talk about past actions and events which happened over a short period or a longer period.
*He **closed** the door and **walked** away.*
*She **lived** in Bratislava until she was nineteen.*

Past continuous
Form

was / were + -ing form of the verb

*She **was listening** to her favourite band.*
*They **were living** in Brighton at the time.*

Use

You use the past continuous to talk about the circumstances around a particular event in the past.

The past continuous is often used in the same sentence with the past simple. The word *when* is often used to combine the two actions in the same sentence.
*I **was driving** home <u>when</u> he **called**.*
*<u>When</u> he **called**, I **was driving** home.*

Unit 3

Expressing necessity and advice

It's necessary to do something – *must / have to*

> *must / have to* + infinitive

You use *must* or *have to* when you feel it is necessary to do something. The two have similar meanings but *must* can only be used to talk about the present and future. The past form is *had to*.
*I haven't spoken to Kate for ages. I **must** call her.*
*I **had to** get up early yesterday. My plane left at six.*

It's necessary not to do something – *mustn't*

> *mustn't* + infinitive

When it is necessary <u>not</u> to do something, you use *mustn't*.
*You **mustn't** do anything that will upset her.*

It's not necessary (i.e. optional) to do something – *don't have to / don't need to*

> *don't have to / don't need to* + infinitive

When you want to say that something is optional, you use *don't have to* or *don't need to*.

You	**don't have to** **don't need to**	come to school tomorrow.

This means 'If you want to come to school, you can, but if you don't want to, that's OK.'

It is / isn't a good idea to do something – *should / ought to / shouldn't*

> *should / ought to / shouldn't* + infinitive

When you want to talk about something you think is or isn't a good idea, or give someone some advice, you use *should, ought to* or *shouldn't*.
*You **should** try to relax more.*
*You **ought to** eat more fruit and vegetables.*
*You **shouldn't** smoke so much.*

Unit 4

Uses of *will*

> *will / won't* + infinitive

You can use *will* in many different ways. Here are some of them:

Promises and offers

I'll take you to the station.
Will you have some tea before you go?
*I **won't** ever marry that awful man!*

Requests and orders

Will you open your books on page 26, please?
I'll have the fish, please.
Will you turn that music down?

Prediction

They'll win 5–0 this weekend.
Will you be warm enough without a jacket?
*You **won't** like Dom – he's hasn't got your sense of humour.*

Other ways of talking about the future

going to

You use *going to* to talk about decisions or intentions in the future, or to predict an event where there is present evidence.
*I'm **going to** be a pilot.*
*I'm **going to** call Tim later.*
*Look out! It's **going to** fall.*

Present continuous

You use the present continuous to talk about things you have arranged to do.
*I'm **meeting** Sue at eight this evening.*
*We're **staying** with friends this weekend.*

Wordlist

*** the 2,500 most common English words, ** very common words, * fairly common words

Unit 1

actor *n* /ˈæktə/ ***
agent *n* /ˈeɪdʒənt/ ***
basketball *n* /ˈbɑːskɪtˌbɔːl/ *
be attracted to *v* /bi əˈtræktɪd tuː, tə/
be into *v* /bi ˈɪntuː, ˈɪntə/
business *n* /ˈbɪznəs/ ***
comedy *n* /ˈkɒmədi/ **
country of origin *n* /ˈkʌntri əv ˈɒrɪdʒɪn/
differently *adv* /ˈdɪfrəntli/ ***
frequently *adv* /ˈfriːkwəntli/ ***
gift *n* /ɡɪft/ ***
go into *v* /ˌɡəʊ ˈɪntuː, ˈɪntə/
grow up *v* /ˌɡrəʊ ˈʌp/
hang out (with friends) *v* /ˌhæŋ aʊt (wɪð ˈfrendz)/
hip-hop *n* /ˈhɪp ˌhɒp/
horror *n* /ˈhɒrə/ **
job opportunities *n pl* /ˈdʒɒb ˌɒpəˌtjuːnətɪz/
karate *n* /kəˈrɑːti/
look after *v* /ˌlʊk ˈɑːftə/
miss *v* /mɪs/ ***
mix (with) *v* /mɪks (wɪð)/ ***
normally *adv* /ˈnɔːməli/ ***
rap *n* /ræp/
reading *n* /ˈriːdɪŋ/ ***
reggae *n* /ˈreɡeɪ/
research *n* /rɪˈsɜːtʃ/ ***
science fiction *n* /ˌsaɪəns ˈfɪkʃn/ *
strict *adj* /strɪkt/ **
supportive *adj* /səˈpɔːtɪv/
take after *v* /ˌteɪk ˈɑːftə/
talent *n* /ˈtælənt/ **
tennis *n* /ˈtenɪs/ **
treat *v* /triːt/ ***
watching TV *n* /ˌwɒtʃɪŋ ˌtiː ˈviː/

Unit 2

be pushed out *v* /bi ˌpʊʃt ˈaʊt/
be valued at *v* /bi ˈvæljuːd ət/ **
brightly-coloured *adj* /ˌbraɪtli ˈkʌləd/
co-founder *n* /ˌkəʊ ˈfaʊndə/
company *n* /ˈkʌmpəni/ ***
do an exam *v* /ˌduː ən ɪɡˈzæm/
do business *v* /ˌduː ˈbɪznəs/
do some damage *v* /ˌduː səm ˈdæmɪdʒ/
do someone a favour *v* /ˌduː ˌsʌmwʌn ə ˈfeɪvə/
do well / badly *v* /ˌduː ˈwel, ˈbædli/
do your homework *v* /ˌduː jɔː ˈhəʊmwɜːk/
drop *v* /drɒp/ ***
full-sized *adj* /ˌfʊl ˈsaɪzd/
gadget *n* /ˈɡædʒɪt/
gizmo *n* /ˈɡɪzməʊ/
go back *v* /ˌɡəʊ ˈbæk/
innovative *adj* /ˈɪnəvətɪv/ *
introduce *v* /ˌɪntrəˈdjuːs/ ***
invent *v* /ɪnˈvent/ **
make a decision *phrase* /ˌmeɪk ə dɪˈsɪʒn/
make a mistake *phrase* /ˌmeɪk ə mɪˈsteɪk/
make a phone call *phrase* /ˌmeɪk ə ˈfəʊnkɔːl/
make money *phrase* /ˌmeɪk ˈmʌni/
make someone angry *phrase* /ˌmeɪk ˌsʌmwʌn ˈæŋɡri/
make someone laugh / cry *phrase* /ˌmeɪk ˌsʌmwʌn ˈlɑːf, kraɪ/
management *n* /ˈmænɪdʒmənt/ ***
meet *v* /miːt/ ***
policy *n* /ˈpɒləsi/ ***
produce *v* /prəˈdjuːs/ ***
recently *adv* /ˈriːsəntli/ ***
retirement *n* /rɪˈtaɪəmənt/ *
return (to) *v* /rɪˈtɜːn (tuː, tə)/ ***
scent *n* /sent/ *
start *v* /stɑːt/ ***
translator *n* /trænsˈleɪtə/
unusual *adj* /ʌnˈjuːʒʊəl/ ***

Unit 3

ability *n* /əˈbɪləti/ ***
attention *n* /əˈtenʃn/ ***
boring *adj* /ˈbɔːrɪŋ/ ***
care (about) *v* /keə (əbaʊt)/ ***
clear *adj* /klɪə/ ***
confident *adj* /ˈkɒnfɪdənt/ **
criticize *v* /ˈkrɪtɪsaɪz/ **
demanding *adj* /dɪˈmɑːndɪŋ/ **
embarrassed *adj* /ɪmˈbærəst/ *
emotion *n* /ɪˈməʊʃn/ ***
energy *n* /ˈenədʒi/ ***
experienced *adj* /ɪkˈspɪəriənst/ **
fall down *v* /ˌfɔːl ˈdaʊn/
friendly *adj* /ˈfrendli/ ***
helpful *adj* /ˈhelpfl/ **
interesting *adj* /ˈɪntrəstɪŋ/ ***
interpret *v* /ɪnˈtɜːprɪt/ ***
kind *adj* /kaɪnd/ ***
nervous *adj* /ˈnɜːvəs/ **
outline *n* /ˈaʊtlaɪn/ **
over-sensitive *adj* /ˌəʊvəˈsensətɪv/
percentage *n* /pəˈsentɪdʒ/ **
pleasant *adj* /ˈpleznt/ **
position *n* /pəˈzɪʃn/ ***
practical *adj* /ˈpræktɪkl/ ***
psychic *adj* /ˈsaɪkɪk/
quiet *adj* /ˈkwaɪət/ ***
reasonable *adj* /ˈriːznəbl/ ***
selfish *adj* /ˈselfɪʃ/ *
sensible *adj* /ˈsensəbl/ **
sensitive *adj* /ˈsensətɪv/ ***
shy *adj* /ʃaɪ/ *
snore *v* /snɔː/
string *n* /strɪŋ/ ***
suspicious *adj* /səˈspɪʃəs/ **
swing *v* /swɪŋ/ ***
symbol *n* /ˈsɪmbl/ **
trust *v* /trʌst/ ***
turn (the lights) down *v* /ˌtɜːn (ðə ˈlaɪts) ˌdaʊn/
upset *adj* /ʌpˈset/ **

Unit 4

abroad *adv* /əˈbrɔːd/ ***
accountant *n* /əˈkaʊntənt/ **
agricultural worker *n* /ˌæɡrɪˈkʌltʃərəl ˌwɜːkə/
aim *n* /eɪm/ ***
analyse *v* /ˈænəlaɪz/ **
architect *n* /ˈɑːkɪtekt/ **
banker *n* /ˈbæŋkə/ *
break *v* /breɪk/ ***
charming *adj* /ˈtʃɑːmɪŋ/ **
computer operator *n* /kəmˈpjuːtər ˌɒpəreɪtə/
computer programmer *n* /kəmˈpjuːtə ˈprəʊɡræmə/
crazy *adj* /ˈkreɪzi/ **
create *v* /kriˈeɪt/ ***
creative *adj* /kriˈeɪtɪv/ **
dangerous *adj* /ˈdeɪndʒərəs/ ***
dentist *n* /ˈdentɪst/ *
designer *n* /dɪˈzaɪnə/ **
developed *adj* /dɪˈveləpt/ *
distribute *v* /dɪˈstrɪbjuːt/ **
energetic *adj* /ˌenəˈdʒetɪk/ *
engineer *n* /ˌendʒɪˈnɪə/ ***
estate agent *n* /əˈsteɪt ˌeɪdʒənt/
fall in love *v* /ˌfɔːl ɪn ˈlʌv/
feed *v* /fiːd/ ***
flight attendant *n* /ˈflaɪt əˌtendənt/
health worker *n* /ˈhelθ ˌwɜːkə/ *
illness *n* /ˈɪlnəs/ ***
lawyer *n* /ˈlɔːjə/ ***
librarian *n* /laɪˈbreəriən/ *
local *adj* /ˈləʊkl/ ***
malaria *n* /məˈleəriə/
mathematician *n* /ˌmæθəməˈtɪʃn/
mechanic *n* /məˈkænɪk/ *

medical supplies *n* /ˈmedɪkl səˌplaɪz/
nurse *n* /nɜːs/ ***
observe *v* /əbˈzɜːv/ ***
offer *v* /ˈɒfə/ ***
organise *v* /ˈɔːɡənaɪz/ ***
original *adj* /əˈrɪdʒn(ə)l/ ***
persuade *v* /pəˈsweɪd/ ***
photographer *n* /fəˈtɒɡrəfə/ **
pilot *n* /ˈpaɪlət/ ***
plumber *n* /ˈplʌmə/ *
politician *n* /ˌpɒləˈtɪʃn/ ***
priest *n* /priːst/ **
professional *adj* /prəˈfeʃnəl/ ***
properly *adv* /ˈprɒpəli/ ***
receptionist *n* /rɪˈsepʃnɪst/ *
routine *n* /ruːˈtiːn/ **
salesperson *n* /ˈseɪlzpɜːsn/
scientific *adj* /ˌsaɪənˈtɪfɪk/ ***
secretary *n* /ˈsekrətri/ ***
service *n* /ˈsɜːvɪs/ **
similar *adj* /ˈsɪmɪlə/ ***
skills *n pl* /skɪlz/ ***
sociable *adj* /ˈsəʊʃəbl/
social *adj* /ˈsəʊʃl/ ***
social worker *n* /ˈsəʊʃl ˌwɜːkə/ ***
solve *v* /sɒlv/ ***
spend (time) *v* /ˌspend (ˈtaɪm)/ ***
superficial *adj* /ˌsuːpəˈfɪʃl/ *
teacher *n* /ˈtiːtʃə/ ***
tool *n* /tuːl/ ***
voluntary *adj* /ˈvɒləntri/ **
volunteer *n* /ˌvɒlənˈtɪə/ **
well-organised *adj* /ˌwel ˈɔːɡənaɪzd/

Communication activities

Unit 2, Speaking Ex 2 page 9

Group 1		Group 2		Group 3	
1	chewing gum	1	schools	1	candles
2	mobile phones	2	trainers	2	pencils
3	zips	3	tuna fish	3	sunglasses
4	horses	4	bottles	4	scissors
5	passports	5	watches	5	iPod
6	contact lenses	6	safety pins	6	paper

Unit 3, Lead-in Ex 2 page 10

Psychic rating

If you scored mostly As: Wow! Your psychic abilities are being used daily. You are definitely in touch with your spiritual side. Is it your job? Meditation helps your mind to stay relaxed and will help your psychic abilities to grow, but of course, you probably already know that.

If you scored mostly Bs: You have kept your natural psychic ability in use. You could easily improve this ability by taking classes on how to develop your psychic skills or just practising yourself. Read about other psychic methods and find the one that suits you.

If you scored mostly Cs: Your psychic abilities have been pushed far to the back of your mind. But they are still there, sleeping. To wake them up, start reading about how you can develop your awareness of the world around you, not only what you can see but also what you can feel.

Unit 4, Vocabulary Ex 4 page 15

1 Work with a partner. Ask him / her the questions and complete the test with his / her answers.

Find your
ideal occupation

1 Which of these do you like? (only tick the ones your partner likes)

A working with tools and machines
B solving science or maths problems
C creating things
D helping people
E offering a professional service to people
F organising numbers and records

2 Do you see yourself as:

A practical?
B scientific?
C creative and original?
D friendly and helpful?
E energetic and sociable?
F well-organised?

3 Which of these don't you like? (only tick the ones your partner doesn't like)

A social activities?
B selling to people or persuading people?
C doing the same thing every day?
D using tools or machines?
E observing or analysing?
F breaking from routine?

2 Which letter or letters A–F did your partner choose most? Turn to page 32 to find out the occupations for his / her personality type(s). Does he / she agree?

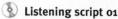

Unit 1 I know what I like

 Listening script 01

Reading text from page 3

 Listening script 02

(B = Ben, L = Layla, I = Ian)
B: Hi. What's your name?
L: Hi. I'm Layla.
B: Nice to meet you, Layla. I'm Ben. So, what do you do?
L: I'm at university at the moment.
B: Me too. What's your subject?
L: Business. It's a bit boring, but the job opportunities are good. What about you?
B: Art and design. It's OK, but I'm more into music, actually.
L: Oh, what sort of music do you like?
B: All sorts, but I'm in a band and we play a mix of reggae and hip-hop stuff. Those are our favourites, anyway.
L: Oh, really? I'm, like, the world's biggest reggae fan.
B: You should come and see us.
L: I'd love to.
B: Good, I'll give you the details later. So, what else do you like doing?
L: Well, um, when I'm not studying, I like hanging out with my friends and (bell rings) oh …
B: I like hanging out with my friends, too. Let's talk a bit more later.
L: OK. See you later.
B: Ciao.
I: Hello, hello. My name's Ian. And you are?
L: Hi, Ian. I'm Layla.
I: Nice to meet you. I work in scientific research. It's very interesting. At the moment, we're working on the DNA of a very …
L: That is interesting. I'm studying business at university.
I: Ah, student days. The happiest days of your life. I remember when I was at university, I …
L: Do you have any hobbies, Ian?
I: I love going to the cinema.
L: Oh, me too. What kind of films do you like?
I: My favourite type of film is science fiction. Do you know I even have a Stormtrooper's uniform from *Star Wars* …
L: I prefer comedies. Science fiction's not really my thing. And horror – I really like that.
I: Yes, I like old comedies. But horror, dear me, no. I can't stand horror films. They are not clever, they are not funny and they are not scary.
L: Oh, I also really like reading. I'm reading a story at the moment about a family living in …
I: Mm, I don't like reading that much. I prefer watching TV to relax. I think (bell rings) … oh, what a shame. I was enjoying that. Um, I'll see you again later, though, I hope.
L: Bye then.

Unit 2 Great minds

 Listening script 03

(I = Interviewer, K = Kathryn Yates)
I: … and on this evening's *Great Minds* we're talking to Kathryn Yates, who has studied the life of the inventor and businessman, Steve Jobs. Kathryn welcome.
K: Thank you. Good to be here.
I: OK, I guess the first question is: who is Steve Jobs?
K: Steve Jobs is co-founder of Apple. He and his friend, Steve Wozniak, invented the personal computer.
I: Wow. A couple of clever guys. How did they meet?
K: They met for the first time when they were working at the same company during the summer holidays. Steve Jobs was just 13 years old and Steve Wozniak was 18. They discovered that they both had the same interests and both had dreams about making the world a better place, and that was the beginning of a great partnership.
I: And later they started to build this personal computer?
K: Right, and when it was finally ready, they named it Apple 1 …
I: By the way, why did they call the company Apple?
K: Well, the story I heard was that Steve Jobs had the idea for a home computer when he was picking apples in an orchard in Oregon. He looked at the apple in his hand and decided to call his future company Apple.
I: Beautiful. So, is this the perfect success story, then?
K: Well, not quite. Apple grew very fast. Three years after they started the company, it was worth $100 million. But soon afterwards the new management pushed Steve out of his own company. You see, Steve Jobs had a different way of thinking and the business people didn't really understand him.
I: Mm, not such a happy ending after all, then?
K: Well, it didn't actually end there. Years later, after trying a few different presidents, the Apple management realised that they needed Steve after all. Steve was making the movie *Toy Story* with his new company, Pixar, when Apple asked him to come back.
I: So he went back?
K: He did.
I: Incredible.
K: Yes, and from the moment he returned he started adding colour to the company. Until 1998, all computers were grey or beige. Steve changed all that with the brightly coloured iMacs. Then came iTunes and the iPod. Apple became a popular company once again.
I: Amazing. Kathryn, can I stop you there for a moment? We're going to take a short break, but join us again in a few moments to hear more about this …

 Listening script 04

Language study Ex 3 from page 7

 Listening script 05

Pronunciation Ex 1 from page 7

 Listening script 06

Pronunciation Ex 2 from page 7

 Listening script 07

Reading text from page 8

 Listening script 08

(T = Teacher, J = José, W = Wanlee)
T: José, what are you going to talk about?
J: Toothbrushes.
T: And Wanlee?
W: Chickens.
T: OK, when you're ready.
J: Toothbrushes are much more important than chickens – you can eat anything: beef, vegetables, fruit, but you can only clean your teeth with one thing – a toothbrush.
W: That's not true. You can brush your teeth with a stick or even with chewing gum, but chickens give us eggs. You can eat eggs, paint with eggs (like Leonardo daVinci), or even throw eggs at politicians. If someone comes to your house, you need eggs to make them a delicious cake …
J: But without toothbrushes you wouldn't have any teeth …

Unit 3 The sixth sense

 Listening script 09

Reading text from page 11

Listening script 10

(N = Newsreader, S = Simon Ward)
N: Can our sleeping position tell us something about our character? According to recent research, yes. Let's go over to our science reporter, Simon Ward, to hear more about it. Simon?
S: Fiona, according to research by Professor Chris Idzikowski, director of the Sleep Assessment and Advisory Service, there are six common sleeping positions and each one is linked to a particular personality type. The most common position is the Foetus. 41% of us sleep in this position, mostly women. A person who sleeps like this is sensitive – they care about others – but they are also quite shy, especially when meeting people for the first time. But people from this group make very good, and loyal, friends.

The next most popular position, for 15% of us, is the Log. It's called the Log because, lying with your arms and legs straight, you look like a fallen tree. These sleepers are friendly and mix easily with others. However, they sometimes think only about themselves and can actually be quite selfish. So, friendly but not always a good friend.

13% of us are Yearners. The sleeping position is like the Log except both arms are out in front of them. These people are sensible, and never do anything too crazy, but they don't trust people easily and tend to be quite suspicious by nature. They are slow to make decisions but once they do, they are unlikely to change them.

If you sleep lying on your back with both arms by your sides, then you are a Soldier. As a Soldier, you are a quiet person and generally speak only when someone speaks to you. However, you expect a lot from other people and you can be difficult to please, in fact rather demanding. Apart from personality, if you sleep in this position you will probably snore.

The Freefaller is a confident person, or certainly seems confident, but they don't like to be criticised and can become quite emotional. This oversensitivity only shows itself in particularly extreme situations.

The Starfish is the final category. These sleepers make good friends and are always ready to offer help. They don't like to be the centre of attention and they are very good listeners. The only negative is that they can be boring and even send you to sleep when talking about their interests. However, if you sleep next to a Starfish, you will probably be woken up by their snoring!

Fiona, back to you.

Unit 4 What do you do?

 Listening script 11

Reading text from page 14

 Listening script 12

(M = Kelly's mum, K = Kelly)
M: Kelly, what would you like to drink?
K: I'll have a cup of tea, please.
M: Come down then.
K: Thanks. Mum, what's wrong?
M: Oh, nothing. I was just thinking about you out there. There are a lot of dangerous animals …
K: Mum, don't start again, please. I'll be OK. I'll be fine, really.
M: Will they feed you properly?
K: I'm sure they will. I get all my meals included. Anyway, it's not me you should worry about. You know, more than 200 children die every week because they don't have enough food or because of malaria …
M: Malaria? You might get malaria?
K: Oh, Mum, I won't. I'm taking anti-malaria tablets and we have all the right medicines. Don't worry, Mum. I'm only going to be there for eight weeks. I'll call you every week. Honestly.
M: You might fall in love and not want to come home.
K: Mummy! Now you're just being embarrassing!

 Listening script 13

1 I'll cut taxes and I'll introduce free health care. You have my word on that.

2 OK, everybody. Will you sit in a circle, please? Sarah? Sarah! Come and sit down now, please.

3 It'll probably take about two hours to fix this pipe. Mmm, you'd better make that three hours.

4 Dentist: Will you open just a little wider, please?
  Patient: Gnngnngnn.
  Dentist: Yes, about 5.30, I think.
  Patient: Gnnngnn … gnngn!

5 Doctor: Your heart's fine – you'll live longer than all of us, Mrs Smith. Mrs Smith? MRS SMITH!
  Mrs Smith: Mm? Oh, sorry, doctor. I think I must have fallen asleep.
  Doctor: Please, never do that to me again, Mrs Smith.

6 Fuel problem? Sure, I'll take a look right now. There's nothing wrong with your car. You've just forgotten to put petrol in it.

 Listening script 14

Yes, I'll get them this afternoon. Yes. Yes, I will. All right … But … but … Will you? OK, thanks … No, I won't. I never do. Don't worry … OK, OK, I'll see you later.

Unit 5 Review

 Listening script 15

(P = Presenter, T = Thomas)
P: Good afternoon and welcome to *Moving On.* Today, I'm talking to Thomas Hunter. Last month, Thomas gave up his job as a computer programmer. He's now planning to spend the next year sailing around the world. Thomas, Hello …

T: Hello.

P: First, tell me – you enjoyed your job, didn't you?

T: Yes, I did. The people I worked with were friendly and interesting.

P: And, I think you were making quite a lot of money …

T: That's right.

P: So, why did you decide to leave?

T: Well, I worked in an office and the truth is that I can't stand being indoors all the time. I like doing sport and other outdoor activities and, in my job, I worked so many hours, I never had any free time. I just wanted to change my life – while I'm still young.

P: I see, and when did you make the decision to go on a trip around the world?

T: It was about two months ago. I was thinking about going on holiday and I was looking on the internet when I saw an advert for a boat. It wasn't very expensive, so I bought the boat and started sailing lessons. There's a lake near my house. Then, on my first lesson, I was sailing across the lake when I had the idea – to go on a trip around the world. So, I went into work the next day and told my manager.

P: Was he shocked?

T: Yes, at first, but I think he knew I'd made the right decision.

P: Do you think you have to be a good sailor to travel so far?

T: Well, I know what I'm doing now. I'm young. I'm fit. I'm a sensible person. I think I'll be fine.

P: You certainly seem very practical, but what about money?

T: I don't need to earn any money for a while.

P: OK, but, you're going on your own. Won't you be lonely?

T: No. I don't think so. I like being on my own.

P: So, what advice would you give to people who don't like their jobs?

T: They should move on, definitely. They should change their jobs or do something else they like. They shouldn't do things they don't want to do.

P: Thank you, Thomas. Will you come and see us when you get back?

T: Of course, and I'll send you a postcard from every country I visit.

P: Thank you. Now let's move on to …

 Listening script 16

Song from page 20

Communication activities

Unit 3, Language study Ex 6 page 12

1 Make questions from the sentences in the table.

Example:
Do you have to wear a uniform at work?

Find someone who ...	Name
1 has to wear a uniform at work.	_____
2 thinks he / she should do more exercise.	_____
3 doesn't have to get up early tomorrow.	_____
4 thinks we shouldn't eat so much junk food.	_____
5 doesn't need to wear glasses to read.	_____
6 feels that he / she must make an effort to keep in touch with his / her friends.	_____
7 thinks he / she ought to give up smoking.	_____
8 agrees that we mustn't cut down any more of the rainforest.	_____

2 Ask other students your questions. Try to find someone different to answer each question and write the name of the person in the table. Find out as much information as you can.

Example:
What do you do? Do you work long hours?

3 Tell the class the most interesting piece of information you found.

Unit 4, Vocabulary Ex 4 page 15

Results of the
ideal occupation test

If you selected mostly ...

As, you are a **Realistic** personality type. Your ideal job would be something working with tools, machines or animals. Jobs in your category include: mechanic, pilot, plumber, engineer and agricultural worker.

Bs, you are an **Investigative** personality type. Your ideal job would be working out mathematical or scientific problems. Jobs in your category include: dentist, mathematician, family doctor and computer programmer.

Cs, you are an **Artistic** personality type. Your ideal job would be working in drama, dance, music or creative writing. Jobs in your category include: actor, photographer, designer, architect, singer and writer.

Ds, you are a **Social** personality type. Your ideal job would be helping, nursing or teaching people. Jobs in your category include: priest, social worker, librarian, nurse and teacher.

Es, you are an **Enterprising** personality type. Your ideal job would be leading people or helping to sell things or ideas. Jobs in your category include: lawyer, politician, salesperson, estate agent, and flight attendant.

Fs, you are a **Conventional** personality type. Your ideal job would be working with numbers, records or machines. Jobs in your category include: accountant, banker, receptionist, secretary and computer operator.

It's very normal to have an equal number in two categories. This means that your options are wider and you can choose from both categories.

Module 2
Taste

Unit	Topic	Language study	Vocabulary	Main skills
1 Don't breathe a word! pages 34–37	• Gossip • You didn't hear it from me	• Talking about recent events (past simple and present perfect simple) • Phrases to talk about time and quantity	• Phrases about friendship and rumour	• **Reading:** identifying key information • **Listening:** completing details of events • **Speaking:** listening and responding to news about other people
2 Pass the popcorn, please pages 38–41	• Mad about movies • Movie mistakes message board	• Asking for and giving opinions	• Types of film • Describing elements of a film	• **Reading:** identifying main ideas • **Listening:** identifying descriptions • **Pronunciation:** emphatic stress in description phrases • **Speaking:** discussing strengths and weaknesses of a film • **Writing:** a film review
3 You must try it pages 42–45	• A question of taste (response to blue food) • Good manners cost nothing (politeness in restaurant conversations) • Doing the right thing (cultural expectations)	• Quantifiers with countable and uncountable nouns	• Food • Ordering food in restaurants	• **Reading:** understanding main ideas • **Speaking:** roleplay between customer and waiter; discussing good and bad manners • **Listening:** identifying correct information
4 Followers of fashion pages 46–49	• Looking good (beauty contest) • Body art	• Recognising and using phrasal verbs	• Describing appearance and things you wear	• **Reading:** identifying main ideas • **Speaking:** discussing beauty and body decoration • **Listening:** understanding descriptions of body art • **Writing:** an email explaining a decision

5 Review unit pages 50–53

• **Extra practice** pages 54–57 • **Grammar reference and wordlist** pages 58–60 • **Listening scripts:** pages 62–63 • **Communication activities:** pages 61, 64

1 Don't breathe a word!

LEARNING AIMS

- Can talk about recent events
- Can use phrases to talk about time and quantity
- Can listen and respond to news about other people

Gossip

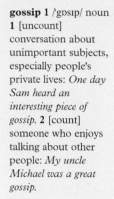

gossip 1 /ˈgɒsɪp/ noun
1 [uncount]
conversation about
unimportant subjects,
especially people's
private lives: *One day
Sam heard an
interesting piece of
gossip.* **2** [count]
someone who enjoys
talking about other
people: *My uncle
Michael was a great
gossip.*

gossip 2 /ˈgɒsɪp/ verb
to talk about other
people or about things
that are not important

Extract from *Macmillan
Dictionary for Advanced Learners*

Lead-in

1 Work in groups. Read the definition of gossip and discuss these questions.

    1   What do you think about gossip? Do you think it's a good or a bad thing? Why?

    2   Do you ever gossip? If so, who do you gossip about and who do you gossip to?

Reading

1 Which of these statements do you agree with? Discuss your opinions with a partner.

    1   People usually spend more time gossiping on the phone than face to face.

    2   Women gossip more than men.

    3   Men and women gossip so that they can feel better about themselves.

    4   Women have better communication skills than men.

2   **17** Read the newspaper article on page 35 about a survey on gossip. According to the opinions expressed in the article, which of the statements in Ex 1 are true?

3 Read the text again and choose the correct alternative.

    1   *Less than a quarter | More than a quarter | About a quarter* of people use their mobiles for work – the rest use them to gossip.

    2   *70% | 75% | 80%* of people gossip on their mobiles at least once a week.

    3   Mobiles have become the *cheapest | number one | most expensive* form of communication.

    4   Just over a *quarter | half | third* of men call their friends to gossip.

    5   Men and women gossip *to make their friendship stronger | the same way | in different ways.*

    6   Some women think that men are *very good | not bad | no good* at gossiping.

4 Work with a partner. Discuss the findings of the survey. Do you agree with them? Why? / Why not?

THE CHANGING
FACE OF GOSSIP

A survey revealed last week that gossiping over the airwaves has taken the place of gossiping over the garden fence. More people are using their mobiles to have a chat rather than speaking face to face.

The survey found that although 17% of people use their mobiles for work, most use them to keep in touch or to gossip. Three quarters gossip on them at least once a week and 40% do so every day. The mobile has become the most popular form of communication. It is now even more popular than the standard telephone or email.

Surprisingly (or maybe not), the study tells us that, on average, men gossip more than women. 27% of men (compared with only 21% of women) said they call up their friends to gossip. At first the men used the phrase 'keep in touch', but when questioned further they admitted it was more to spread rumours and gossip.

The study says that men and women gossip differently. Women gossip mainly to form a bond with one another, to make their friendship stronger. Men gossip to feel better about themselves, especially when they complain about another person's behaviour.

But some women have complained this week that men don't understand how to keep a secret or gossip properly. 'They've taken first prize in gossiping but they still don't know how to do it. They don't realise that they need to keep saying "No – really?" and "You're joking!" to encourage the person telling them gossip,' said one woman.

Vocabulary

1 Match the two halves to make phrases. Check your answers in the text.

1 keep	rumours
2 have	a chat
3 spread	in touch
4 form	a secret
5 keep	a bond

2 Look at the phrases in Ex 1. Which one is negative?

3 Replace the underlined words in these sentences with a phrase from Ex 1.

1 My friends tell me their private things because they know I can <u>stay quiet</u>.
2 I usually call my best friend every day to <u>have an informal conversation</u>.
3 I really should make more of an effort to <u>stay in contact</u> with my friends.
4 I never <u>tell stories that I've heard about other people</u>, but I love hearing them.
5 I often share secrets – it's a good way to <u>develop a friendship</u>.

4 Which sentences in Ex 3 are true for you?

5 Work with a partner and discuss these questions. Find out as much as you can from each other.

1 When did you last have a chat with your best friend? What did you talk about?
2 How good are you at keeping in touch with your friends?
3 Have you ever formed a bond with someone after knowing them a short time?
4 Are you good at keeping secrets or do you usually tell someone else?
5 In your opinion, what sort of people spread rumours?

LANGUAGE STUDY

Talking about recent events

Past simple and present perfect simple

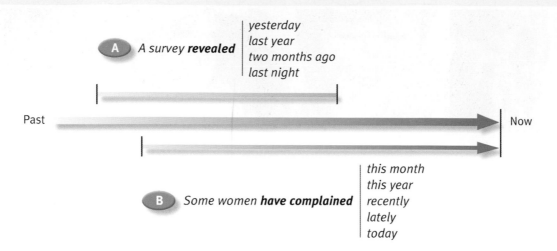

A A survey **revealed** | yesterday / last year / two months ago / last night

Past — Now

B Some women **have complained** | this month / this year / recently / lately / today

1   Look at the diagram and the example sentences. Answer these questions by writing *A* or *B* in the boxes.

   1   Both sentences refer to past actions, but which is:

     •   in a finished time period? ☐

     •   in an unfinished time period? ☐

   2   Which is an example of:

     •   the past simple ☐

     •   the present perfect simple ☐

2   How is the present perfect simple formed?

3   Can you remember the past simple and the present perfect forms of these irregular verbs?

become	break	buy	eat	fall	have	hear	see	speak	take

Grammar reference page 58

4   Read this dialogue. Which of the sentences are about something which happened in a finished time period (A) and which are about something which happened in an unfinished time period (B)? Give reasons for your answers.

Katie: (1) I haven't seen Lindy this week.
Eleni: (2) I saw her last week. (3) She's dyed her hair recently.
Katie: (4) Is that why she hasn't been to class lately?
Eleni: (5) Yes. She missed class on Tuesday and Wednesday, didn't she?

Example: *1 B – because it's still this week.*

5   Choose the correct alternative, according to the diagram in Ex 1.

   1   *Did you do* / *Have you done* any exercise this week?

   2   *Did you get* / *Have you got* home after midnight last night?

   3   *Did you hear* / *Have you heard* any good gossip recently?

   4   *What did you do* / *What have you done* last weekend?

   5   *Did you see* / *Have you seen* any good films lately?

6   Work with a partner. Ask and answer the questions in Ex 5.

7 Complete these sentences with the past simple or present perfect simple form of the verbs.

1 I (eat) __'ve eaten__ in a restaurant four times this month.

2 I (see) _____ two films at the cinema last month.

3 I (have) _____ four meals yesterday.

4 I (buy) _____ five items of clothing this week.

5 I last (go) _____ to the dentist two months ago.

6 I (make) _____ six phone calls today.

8 Change the number in each sentence so that it is true for you.

Example: *I've eaten in a restaurant **three** times this month.*

9 Compare your sentences with a partner. Find out more details from each other.

Example: *I've been to three different restaurants: an Italian, a Chinese and a Mexican. I enjoyed them all, but the Italian was my favourite.*

You didn't hear it from me

Listening and speaking

1 🔘 **18** Listen to two phone conversations (between Nick and Justin, and Ashley and Lisa). Tick (✓) the names of the people they mention.

| Mika ☐ | Natasha ☐ | Ben ☐ | Sara ☐ | Tony ☐ | Marco ☐ |

2 Write the name of each person in the 'Who' column to make complete sentences.

Who	**What**
1 _____	has had a baby.
2 _____	left her job.
3 _____	split up with his girlfriend.
4 _____	has put on weight.

3 Listen again and check your answers to Ex 2. Then match these time expressions to each person's news.

| last week   recently   today   yesterday |

4 What is the connection between: a   Mika and Ben?   b   Sara and Marco?

5 Complete the lists using the phrases in the box.

| ~~According to~~   Apparently   ~~Guess what?~~   Have you heard?   Wow!
I heard that …   ~~No! Really?~~   You're joking!   You won't believe this! |

Introducing some news	Saying it came from someone else	Reacting
Guess what?	*According to*	*No! Really?*

6 Work with a partner. Write a dialogue containing at least two pieces of gossip. Use the topics in Ex 2 (or choose your own) and the phrases in Ex 5.

7 Act out your dialogue in front of the class. Take a class vote on the best gossips.

CD-ROM   For more activities go to **Taste Unit 1**

2 Pass the popcorn, please

LEARNING AIMS

- • Can ask for and give opinions
- • Can write a film review
- • Can describe different elements of a film

Mad about movies

Lead-in

1 Look at the pictures and say what type of film each one is. Use the words in the box to help you.

| animation | comedy | fantasy | gangster movie | historical drama | horror |
| martial arts | romance | science fiction | war drama | western | |

2 Think of a film for each of the types in Ex 1. Compare your ideas with other students.

3 Work in groups and discuss these questions.

1 How often do you go to the cinema?
2 What kind of films do you like watching?
3 Who's your favourite actor?
4 Is there an actor that you don't like? Who and why not?
5 What's your favourite film?

Reading

1 🎧 **19** Read the film review on page 39 about *The Aviator*. How many types of film from Lead-in Ex 1 are mentioned?

2 Read the text again. How are these people connected to Howard Hughes?

1 Martin Scorsese
2 Michael Drosnin
3 Leonardo DiCaprio
4 Katharine Hepburn

3 According to the text, are these statements true or false?

1 Leonardo DiCaprio plays the main character in the film.
2 Howard Hughes worked for the government.
3 Hughes was very rich.
4 Hughes was a film director and a pilot.
5 As a young man, Hughes didn't have many friends.
6 As an old man, Hughes didn't have many friends.

4 What does the reviewer think of the film? Which parts of the text support your view?

5 Find these words in the text and complete the questions.

| biography | convincingly | devote | hesitation | role |

1 Would you like someone to write your _____ one day?
2 Do you think that the leading _____ in a film should always be played by a well-known actor?
3 If someone offered you a ticket to Universal Studios, would you accept without _____?
4 Can you lie _____, or do you always have to tell the truth?
5 Do you feel you have enough time to _____ to your interests?

6 Think about how you would answer the questions in Ex 5. Work with a partner. Ask and answer the questions.

7 Work in groups and discuss these questions.

1 Can you think of any other films you've seen about real people's lives?
2 Were they: **a** accurate? **b** interesting?
3 What did you learn about the person?

MOVIE TIME

THE AVIATOR

Directed by Martin Scorsese, starring Leonardo DiCaprio and Cate Blanchett

There are so many strange stories about Howard Hughes that Martin Scorsese can only tell a small part of it in just two hours and 49 minutes. *The Aviator* won five Oscars but, according to Michael Drosnin, who wrote the best-selling **biography** *Citizen Hughes*, 'The Aviator is a horror movie without the monster -- the real Howard Hughes is not in it.'

I agree with Drosnin. Leonardo DiCaprio, who plays the **role** of Hughes in the film, does not have the power and charisma of the real Howard Hughes. You have to remember that this was a man who bought businesses, property and even governments without a moment's **hesitation**.

In the film he inherits his father's company and becomes the richest young man in the United States. He then moves to Hollywood and becomes a film-maker, producing the war drama *Hell's Angels*, the comedy *The Front Page*, the gangster movie *Scarface* and the western *The Outlaw*.

The Aviator only deals with a part of Hughes' life, from the 1920s to the 1940s -- the most glamorous period of his life. During this period Hughes had many friends, and he had love affairs with many of the most famous actresses of the time, like Ava Gardner and Katharine Hepburn. Kate Beckinsale and Cate Blanchett play the roles of the two stars **convincingly**.

This was also the period of time when he became very interested in flying, and **devoted** more of his time to designing and flying aeroplanes.

Drosnin says that in order to understand Hughes, it is necessary to see him descend into corruption and madness as he gets older. In the final years of his life, Hughes became a paranoid recluse*, with 20 cm long fingernails and dirty, long hair. But the movie does not deal with this part of his life. Instead, and unfortunately in my opinion, Scorsese has chosen only to remember the younger Hughes' spirit of adventure as an aviator.

Glossary
*recluse = someone who lives alone and avoids seeing other people

Listening and pronunciation

1 **20** Jack, Chloe and Ralph have just watched a film together. Listen to their conversation. What was each person's opinion of the film?

2 Listen again. Who or what were these adjectives used to describe? Choose from the items in the box.

the action scenes	the film	Johnny Depp	the special effects

1 fantastic   5 brilliant
2 funny and gorgeous   6 spectacular
3 childish and not funny   7 good
4 impressive

3 Which of these adverbs were used with each adjective in Ex 2?

absolutely	pretty	really	so	very

4 **21** Listen and practice saying the adverbs and adjectives together. Pay particular attention to the intonation.

LANGUAGE STUDY

Asking for and giving opinions

1 Look at phrases a–i from Jack, Chloe and Ralph's conversation. Which are examples of:

1 asking for an opinion?   3 agreeing with an opinion?
2 preparing to give an opinion?   4 not agreeing with an opinion?

a *What did you think of it?*   d *As far as I'm concerned ...*   g *Really?*
b *In my opinion ...*   e *I think ...*   h *If you ask me, ...*
c *Same here.*   f *Me too.*   i *Oh, come on!*

Grammar reference page 58

2 **22** Complete this dialogue by re-ordering the letters in italics. Listen and check your answers.

A: *atwh od uyo nithk fo* (1) _____ Leonardo DiCaprio?

B: I *kinht* (2) _____ he's gorgeous.

C: *em oto.* (3) _____.

A: *larely? Fi ouy kas em,* (4) _____, Johnny Depp is more interesting.

C: Ooh, *asme reeh.* (5) _____. I prefer him, actually.

B: *ho, emoc no* (6) _____! Johnny Depp's too old now.

A: *sa arf sa m'I necconder* (7) _____, they both are.

3 **23** Complete this dialogue. Listen and check your answers.

A: What do you (1) _____ _____ *Hollywood movies?*

B: (2) _____ _____ opinion, *they're boring.*

A: (3) _____? I (4) _____ *they're fantastic.*

B: If (5) _____ _____ me, *Spanish films are much better.*

A: Oh, (6) _____ on! *You see the same actors in every film.*

B: *True, but the acting is really great.*

4 Work with a partner. Prepare and practise your own dialogue, replacing the words in italics in Ex 3 with your own ideas.

5 Turn to page 61 and discuss the opinions.

Vocabulary

1   Look at this message board. After his conversation with Chloe and Jack, Ralph posted a message about the film. Which message is it? Look at listening script 20 on page 62 to help you.

2   Which do you think is the worst mistake? Why? Discuss your ideas with a partner.

Extract from Whoops! Movie Goofs

Movie mistakes message board

The Lord of the Rings (fantasy epic)
Near the end of the film, when Frodo and Sam are talking about their journey, there is a **close-up** on the face of Frodo, and of his contact lenses. Did they have those in Middle Earth?

Minority Report (sci-fi)
The eyes Tom Cruise's **character** receives are from a Japanese/Asian man called Mr Yakamoto in the movie. But how many Asians have got blue eyes?

Reservoir Dogs (gangster drama)
As Mr Pink (**played by** Steve Buscemi) is running away from the police down the street; he runs past the same shop (called HOME CENTER) twice. Then the police following him do the same thing.

Spiderman (fantasy action)
In the **scene** where Peter gets ready for school, he puts on his backpack, and grabs his coat. When the camera shows him outside the door, his coat is on under his backpack.

Pirates of the Caribbean (comedy)
The film was **set** in the Caribbean in the 1600s. In one scene a cannon shot explodes. This is impossible because shells that exploded weren't invented until the mid-1800s.

Gladiator (historical drama)
In the scene where Maximus, Juba and Hagen are eating, someone **in the background** asks about a radio. Er, I don't think radios had been invented in 180 AD.

3   Find these words in the message board and complete the questions.

character	close-up	in the background	played by	scene	set

1   In which films does a _____ of the main _____ reveal a problem with the eyes?

2   Which films are _____ in the past?

3   Which role is _____ Steve Buscemi? What's the film?

4   Which film contains a _____ where a bag changes position?

5   In *Gladiator*, someone _____ asks about a radio. Why is this strange?

4   Answer the questions in Ex 3.

Speaking and writing

1   You are going to interview a partner. Read the instructions and prepare questions and your own answers. Then interview each other.

1   Ask your partner about a film that he / she knows and would like to talk about.
2   Find out what type of film it is.
3   Ask about the main characters in the film.
4   Find out which time and place the film is set in.
5   Find out the main story (the plot) of the film.
6   Ask your partner about the acting, the soundtrack (music) and the special effects.
7   Ask if your partner would recommend this film.

2   Write a review about the film you have just described. Use the ideas in Ex 1 to help you.

3   Find students who have written about a film that you've seen. Do you agree with their reviews?

CD-ROM   For more activities go to **Taste Unit 2**

3 You must try it

LEARNING AIMS

- Can use quantifiers to talk about food
- Can order food in restaurants
- Can discuss good and bad manners

A question of taste

Lead-in 1 Think about the meal you had last night. Discuss these questions.

1 What did you eat?
2 Did it look good?
3 Did it taste good?
4 What colour was the food that you ate?

Reading 1 **24** Read the report about the relationship between colour and the taste of food. Which item in the pictures is not mentioned?

2 Complete these statements about the report.

1 Nature makes food look more attractive so that we want …
2 Some companies add colour to their food so that it looks …
3 Food that is naturally blue, black or purple can sometimes be …
4 The colour blue is often used to help people …
5 In the test, the group with the masks ate more …

3 Work in groups and discuss these questions.

1 Do you think you could you eat a whole plate of blue spaghetti, or would the colour put you off?
2 Have you ever refused to eat something because it didn't look nice? What?

Blue food

Nature's way of making food attractive is to colour it so that it looks delicious. How many vegetables are green? Most of them. How much meat is red? Most of it. We expect our food to come in familiar colours.

Food companies sometimes need to add colour to their products to make them more natural-looking. Margarine, for example, is actually a clear white colour when it's made. Yellow colouring is added to make it look more like butter. We think that it tastes better, although the taste hasn't changed at all.

The colour blue isn't often found in natural food. There aren't any blue vegetables and there isn't any blue meat. As a result, we don't have an automatic desire to eat blue food. A million years ago, when our ancestors searched for food, blue, purple and black were 'warning' colours that the food may be poisonous.

As blue suppresses the appetite, it is used to help a lot of people who want to lose weight. Diet specialists advise people to eat off blue plates and to use knives, forks and spoons with blue handles.

We did our own test to see if colouring food blue affects taste and appetite. Using natural food colouring, we made some blue biscuits, some blue spaghetti and some blue rice. We also made some normal-coloured biscuits, spaghetti and rice. We divided twenty people into two groups, A and B. Group A wore masks. Each person had two bowls in front of them, one with the natural food and one with the coloured food. The results were clear. Most people in Group B, the group who could see what they were eating, said that the blue food tasted different to the normal-coloured food. Nobody in Group A, the group with the masks, noticed any difference in taste. At the end of the test, there were a few biscuits and there was a little pasta left in Group A's bowls, whereas in Group B's, there was a lot of food left, and most of it was blue.

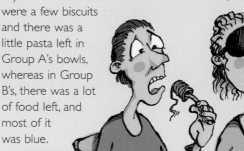

LANGUAGE STUDY

Quantifiers with countable and uncountable nouns

1 Look at these sentences from the text and answer the questions.

How many vegetables are green? *How much meat is red?*

1 Do you use *many* with countable or uncountable nouns?

2 Do you use *much* with countable or uncountable nouns?

2 Look at the text again and <u>underline</u> examples of the words in the box. Are they used with countable nouns, uncountable nouns, or both?

a few   a little   a lot of   any   some

3 Complete the Phrases section of the table using the words in Ex 2.

		Phrases	Nouns
Countable	?	How many?	*vegetables*
	–	There aren't _____	_____
	+	There are _____ / _____ / _____	_____
Uncountable	?	How much?	*margarine*
	–	There isn't _____	_____
	+	There is _____ / _____ / _____	_____

4 Complete the Nouns section of the table. Use some of the items in the pictures in Reading Ex 1 on page 42. Compare your answers with other students.

Grammar reference pages 58 and 59

5 Complete these sentences using *much* or *many*.

1 How _____ people are there in your family?

2 How _____ money could you live on?

3 How _____ time did you spend studying last night?

4 How _____ times have you taken a holiday this year?

5 How _____ meals do you usually eat in a day?

6 Work with a partner. Ask and answer the questions in Ex 5. Answer four questions truthfully and answer one untruthfully. Can your partner guess which answer is untrue?

7 You are going to prepare a meal for some friends. You need to check if you have all the ingredients you need in the house. Student A turn to page 61. Student B turn to page 64.

8 Complete these sentences using *a little*, *a few* or *a lot of* to make them true for you.

1 I've got _____ really close friends.

2 In the evenings, I spend _____ time watching TV.

3 I've been to the cinema _____ times in the last six months.

4 I've written _____ emails this week.

5 I usually add _____ salt to my food.

9 Work in groups. Tell each other your sentences from Ex 8 and find out more details.

Example:

A: *I've got a few really close friends.*

B: *Really? How often do you see them?*

A: *I see most of them every day.*

Good manners cost nothing

The test of good manners is to be patient with bad ones. Solomon ben Yehuda ibn Gabirol

Vocabulary **1** 🔘 **25** Read and listen to this conversation in a restaurant. What does the waiter think of the customer?

A: (1) I want to eat.
B: Certainly, sir. Have you booked?
A: (2) No.
B: No problem. Would you come this way, please?
A: (3) Menu.
B: Of course, sir. I'll get you one immediately.

B: Are you ready to order?
A: (4) Mm.
B: Any starters?
A: (5) No. Bring me a big plate of spaghetti.
B: Main course. Certainly. Anything else?
A: (6) No. (7) Oh, hey you! I'm thirsty!
B: I'll bring you another bottle, sir.

B: Would you like any dessert, or coffee?
A: (8) No. I want to pay.
B: Certainly. That'll be £12.50, please.
A: (9) Here's fifteen. And I want the change!
B: And here's your change, sir. … What a horrible man. He didn't even leave a tip.

2 Improve the customer's manners. Replace his comments with these comments.

> I'll just have the spaghetti, please.   Yes, please.   Could I see the menu, please?
> I'd like a table for one, please.   No, thanks.   Just the bill, please.   No, I haven't.
> Oh, excuse me, could I have some more water, please?   Here you are. Thanks.

3 🔘 **26** Listen and check your answers. What did the waiter think of him this time? What is a *tip*?

4 Match the two halves to make sentences. Who says each one, the customer or the waiter?

1	Hello? I'd like to book	a	I can recommend the avocado.
2	I don't understand any of this –	b	and who ordered steak?
3	For starters,	c	a table for two, please.
4	I'll just have a main	d	bill, please.
5	Who wanted the fish,	e	do you have a menu in English?
6	Would you like any	f	change. Thank you very much.
7	Just the	g	dessert? Or coffee?
8	And here's your	h	course, please.

5 Work with a partner. Act out a conversation between a customer and a waiter in a restaurant. Use the conversation in Ex 2 and the sentences in Ex 4 to help you.

Doing the right thing

Listening and speaking

1 Work with a partner. Look at these pieces of advice about good manners when eating around the world. Complete each by choosing *a*, *b* or *c*.

1 At a formal dinner in North America, with several sets of knives and forks, it is customary to:
  a use the knife and fork on the outside first.
  b use the knife and fork on the inside first.
  c use any knife and fork in any order you like.

2 In China, when not using your chopsticks, it is usual to leave them:
  a sticking into your rice.
  b resting across your plate.
  c resting on the table next to your plate.

3 When you are invited to eat at someone's home in Tunisia, you should:
  a pick up your food with your right hand.
  b pick up your food with your left hand.
  c never pick up your food with your hands.

4 When serving tea from a pot in Britain:
  a you should put the milk into the cup first and then add the tea.
  b you should put the tea into the cup first and then add the milk.
  c you can put the milk or tea in the order you prefer.

5 In Japan, it is all right to make a noise when:
  a eating rice.   b eating noodles.   c eating raw fish

6 In most European countries, taking a bottle of wine to dinner:
  a is a common way of saying 'thank you for inviting me'.
  b will offend your host.
  c is important, but you should take flowers and a dessert, too.

7 Your host won't be happy at a barbecue in Australia if you:
  a dress too casually.
  b wait politely for someone to offer you food.
  c speak to people too informally.

2 🔘 **27** Listen and check your answers. Did any of the answers surprise you? Which ones?

3 Work in groups and discuss these questions.
  1 What kind of food do you like (Italian, Japanese, Chinese, Indian, etc.)?
  2 Is there any food you just can't eat?
  3 Do you get offended by other people's bad manners when you eat with them? Give examples.
  4 How are eating manners in your country different from other countries?

 **CD-ROM**   For more activities go to **Taste Unit 3**

4 Followers of fashion

Based on *Planet Party: A World of Celebration* by Iain Gately

LEARNING AIMS

- Can recognise and use phrasal verbs
- Can discuss beauty and body decoration
- Can write a short email explaining a decision

Looking good

Lead-in   **1**   Which of these statements do you agree with? Discuss your ideas in groups.

1   Beauty contests are really silly. People take them too seriously.
2   I love watching beauty contests. They're great fun.
3   There is no place for beauty contests in today's world. They are old-fashioned and sexist.

Reading   **1**   **28**   Read this book extract about an African beauty contest and find out:

a   who the contestants are   b   who the judges are

BEAUTY
CONTEST

Superficial, sexy, superb: at the Gerewol dance contest, physical beauty is all you need.

Every year the Wodaabe, a tribe of West African nomads, meet to **show off** their most **beautiful** young men in a beauty contest which lasts for seven days. The festival is called Gerewol. During the week, young Wodaabe men parade and dance in front of the women of the tribe.

Early in the morning on the first day of the festival, a woman sings a song to the young men, telling them to get up and prepare to dance.

Before the main dance, the contestants take hours to dress up. They **make up** their faces with a special yellow powder. Then they tie charms around their necks, and put on long, colourful tunics. They **put** turbans **on** their heads, and add a single ostrich feather.

Although the costume is mainly **traditional**, the contestants are happy to try on any new **accessories** that will make them look different, or **trendy**. Some will hang brightly-coloured **watches** on their **necklaces** to make them look more **up-to-date**.

During the dance, the young men roll their eyes and show their perfect teeth with wide smiles, hoping to attract the judges' attention. The judges are three beautiful young women chosen from different Wodaabe tribes. They choose the most original and best-looking dancers as winners. A man who can roll one eye and smile at the same time is considered especially **attractive**.

When a winner is chosen, his people celebrate – it is a great honour to win Gerewol. He will become famous and can expect many wives.

Contests which judge beauty alone have gone out of fashion in the west. In Miss World, the female contestants must show that their personality is as interesting as their looks. Gerewol, in contrast, focuses only on good looks. The Wodaabe believe that beauty exists for a short time and that it is a gift for young people; and while they have the gift, they should parade it for everyone to enjoy.

2 Answer these questions. Then read the text again and check your answers.

1 How long does Gerewol last?
2 Who do the men dance for?
3 What do the contestants put on their faces?
4 What do they put around their necks?
5 When they are dancing, what do the contestants do to attract attention?
6 What does a winner usually get?
7 What is more important in Gerewol – looks or personality?

3 In what ways is Gerewol similar to or different from other beauty contests you know about? Discuss your ideas with a partner. (Think about who competes, how long they last, what the contestants wear, how they prepare and what they win.)

Vocabulary and speaking

1 Put these words from the text into the correct list.

~~accessories~~ attractive beautiful necklace traditional trendy up-to-date watch

Things you wear	Describing appearance
accessories	

2 Add these words to the lists in Ex 1. Then answer the questions.

casual conservative earrings glasses old-fashioned scruffy skirt smart socks tie trousers

1 In *Things you wear*, which would you normally expect to be worn by:
   a a man?   b a woman?   c a man or a woman?

2 In *Describing appearance*, which adjectives mean:
   a fashionable?   b good-looking?

3 In *Describing appearance*, which adjectives have:
   a positive?   b negative?   c neutral meanings?

3 Work in groups and discuss these questions.

1 How would you describe your own style?
2 What are the next three items of clothing that you are going to buy?
3 Which jewellery / accessories do you like? Which would you never wear?
4 Is fashion for all ages, or just the young? Give reasons for your answer.

LANGUAGE STUDY

Recognising and using phrasal verbs

1 Look at these sentences from the text on page 46. Underline the phrasal verbs.

1 *A woman sings a song to the young men, telling them to get up and prepare to dance.*
2 *Before the main dance, the contestants take hours to dress up.*
3 *The contestants are happy to try on any new accessories.*

2 What do you think each phrasal verb means? Discuss your ideas with a partner.

3 Complete the examples in these dictionary entries. Use the phrasal verbs in Ex 1.

1 (I) to wear clothes that are more formal than the clothes you usually wear.
   Example: *He made an effort to _____ for the occasion.*

2 (T) to wear a piece of clothing to see how it looks.
   Example: *What a lovely shirt – why don't you _____ it _____?*

3 (I) to get out of bed after sleeping.
   Example: *He never _____ before nine.*

4 Look at this diagram. Which steps have you followed in Ex 1 to 3?

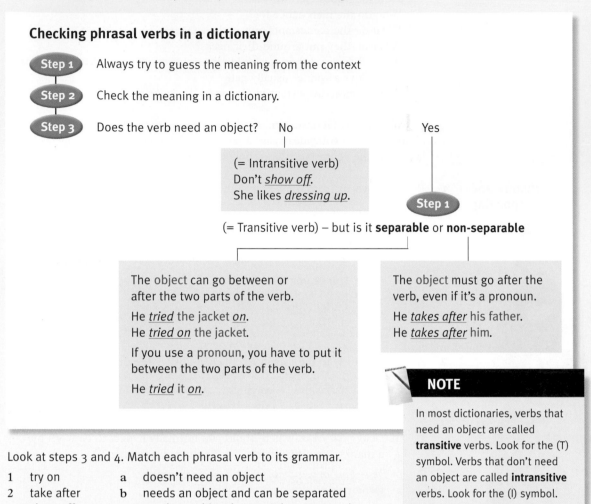

Checking phrasal verbs in a dictionary

Step 1 Always try to guess the meaning from the context

Step 2 Check the meaning in a dictionary.

Step 3 Does the verb need an object?   No   Yes

(= Intransitive verb)
Don't *show off*.
She likes *dressing up*.

Step 1

(= Transitive verb) – but is it **separable** or **non-separable**

The object can go between or after the two parts of the verb.

He *tried* the jacket *on*.
He *tried on* the jacket.

If you use a pronoun, you have to put it between the two parts of the verb.

He *tried* it *on*.

The object must go after the verb, even if it's a pronoun.

He *takes after* his father.
He *takes after* him.

NOTE

In most dictionaries, verbs that need an object are called **transitive** verbs. Look for the (T) symbol. Verbs that don't need an object are called **intransitive** verbs. Look for the (I) symbol.

5 Look at steps 3 and 4. Match each phrasal verb to its grammar.

1	try on	a	doesn't need an object
2	take after	b	needs an object and can be separated
3	show off	c	needs an object but can't be separated

Grammar reference page 59

6 Find and <u>underline</u> these phrasal verbs in the text on page 46: *show off, make up, put on*. What do you think they mean? Mime them with your partner.

7 Look at these sentences and guess the meaning of the phrasal verbs in italics (step 1). Check the meaning in a dictionary or with your teacher (step 2).

1 We were just talking about Joe when we *came across* him in the park.
2 My car was so old I couldn't sell it, so I *gave* it *away*.
3 Only two people can come to the meeting, so I think we should *call it off*.
4 I couldn't come out last night because of my little sister. I had to *look after* her.
5 Joe's always late for work. He didn't *turn up* until ten o'clock this morning.
6 I'm sorry I'm late. It's my stupid alarm clock – it didn't *go off* this morning.

8 Look at the phrasal verbs in Ex 7 again. Which verbs (steps 3 and 4):

a don't need an object?
b need an object and can be separated?
c need an object but can't be separated?

9 Put the pronouns in the correct position in these sentences, only where necessary.

1 Our cat had six kittens. We didn't want any more cats so we gave away. (them)
2 We had to wait for half an hour before he turned up. (him)
3 Oh, this watch is quite old. I came across on eBay. (it)
4 The alarm on my mobile has gone crazy. It went off at four o'clock this morning. (it)
5 If it rains, we can't play the match against Sal and Fran. We'll have to call off. (it)
6 Don't invite Kate tomorrow – I'll have to look after all day and I don't want to. (her)

▲ piercing   ▲ body painting   ▲ henna   ▲ mohican

Body art

Listening and speaking

1 Work in groups. Look at these photos and discuss the questions.

   1   Which of these forms of body art do you think are beautiful?
   2   Which of them would you never try? Why not?
   3   Which of them would you consider trying?

2 🔘 **29** Ellen is having a tattoo done. The tattooist knows a lot about the history of tattooing. Listen to their conversation. Which tattoo is not mentioned?

3 Choose the correct alternative according to the tattooist. Listen again and check your answers.

   1   Tattoos have been around for *2,000 / 3,500 / 5,500* years.
   2   The word 'tattoo' comes from the Tahitian word *tatau / tutu / tonto*.
   3   Captain James Cook was in the South Pacific in *1717 / 1770 / 1870*.
   4   In early Rome, *criminals / sailors / old people* wore tattoos.
   5   In Japan, having a small tattoo means you are *in the mafia / trendy / foreign*.
   6   Ellen's tattoo is photo *2 / 3 / 4*.

4 🔘 **30** Each of these tattoos belongs to one of these well-known people. Can you match them? Listen and check your answers. Then turn to page 64.

   a   singer Pink   c   actress Angelina Jolie   c   actor Johnny Depp
   b   footballer David Beckham   d   singer Robbie Williams

5 Work in groups and discuss these questions.

   1   In your country, are tattoos in fashion or have they gone out of fashion?
   2   If you could have a tattoo for just one day, which design would you choose?

Writing

1 You are going to write an email to a friend and tell him / her that you have decided to have one of the following:

   •   a new (and very different) hairstyle   •   a piercing
   •   cosmetic surgery   •   a tattoo

2 Write your email. Use these ideas to help you.

   1   Tell your friend:
       •   what you've decided to have.
       •   why you've decided to have it.
       •   what your family and friends think of your decision.
   2   Ask your friend what he / she thinks of your decision.

🖱 **CD-ROM**   For more activities go to **Taste Unit 4**

5 Review

Lead-in 1 Work with a partner and discuss these questions. Find out if you have similar tastes.

    1 Do you like going to the cinema or do you prefer to watch DVDs at home? What do you think of the films in the cinema right now?

    2 How often do you eat in restaurants? What kind of food do you prefer?

    3 How important is fashion? Why?

Vocabulary

1   ◉ **31** Listen to three friends having a conversation about taste. Which subjects do they mention?

art ☐	fashion ☐	film ☐	food ☐	gossip ☐	music ☐	sport ☐

2 Listen again and answer these questions. Write *Maya*, *Hannah* or *Josh*. Sometimes there is more than one possible answer.

Who …
1 likes comedies?
2 often talks on the phone?
3 isn't interested in fashion?
4 likes fruit and vegetables?
5 likes fast food?
6 enjoys gossip?

3 Choose the correct alternative. Look at listening script 31 on page 63 to check your answers.

    1 We *formed / made / completed* a strong bond early on.

    2 Do you keep *in / on / at* touch?

    3 We usually have a *talk / chat / speak* on the phone.

    4 She wears *up- / on- / in-* to-date clothes.

    5 She looks *pretty / really / absolutely* fantastic.

    6 I wear *smart / scruffy / casual* jeans all the time.

    7 She can *stay / continue / keep* a secret.

4 Put these words in the correct list.

> absolutely attractive brilliant casual character comedy funny
> gorgeous impressive played by really romance scene set smart so
> trendy very

Film words: _____

Adjectives: _____

Adverbs: _____

5 Complete the information about a TV programme (e.g. a soap opera) that you really like. Use the words in Ex 4 to help you. Tell a partner about your TV programme.

Name of programme:	_____
What the programme is about:	_____
Reasons why you like the programme:	_____
Favourite character:	_____
Reasons why you like the character:	_____
Favourite scene:	_____
Reasons why you like the scene:	_____

Language study

1 Work in small groups. Read how to play 'Party', then play the game.

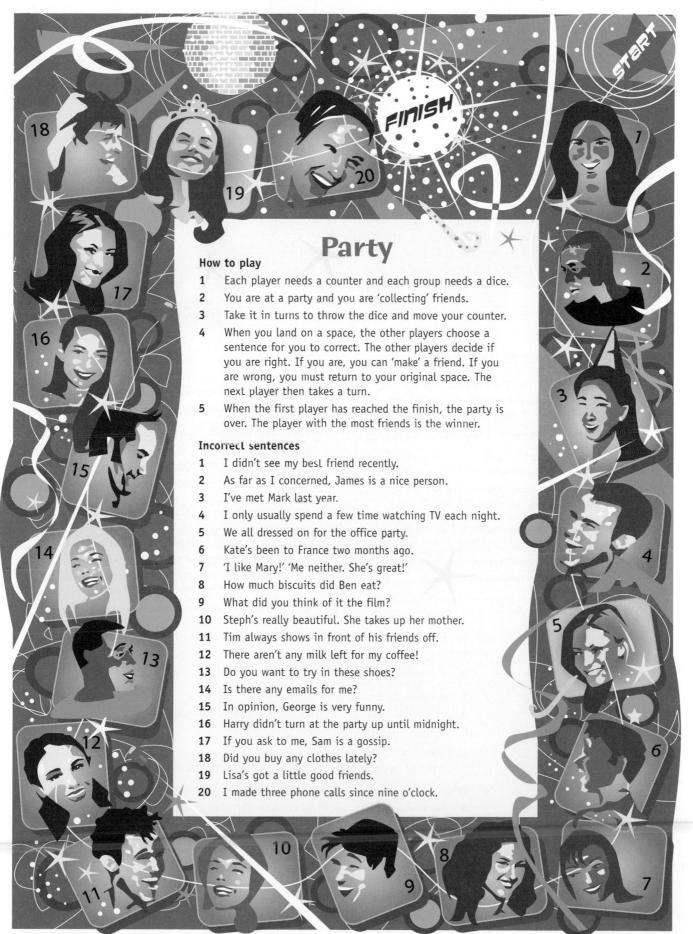

Party

How to play

1 Each player needs a counter and each group needs a dice.
2 You are at a party and you are 'collecting' friends.
3 Take it in turns to throw the dice and move your counter.
4 When you land on a space, the other players choose a sentence for you to correct. The other players decide if you are right. If you are, you can 'make' a friend. If you are wrong, you must return to your original space. The next player then takes a turn.
5 When the first player has reached the finish, the party is over. The player with the most friends is the winner.

Incorrect sentences

1 I didn't see my best friend recently.
2 As far as I concerned, James is a nice person.
3 I've met Mark last year.
4 I only usually spend a few time watching TV each night.
5 We all dressed on for the office party.
6 Kate's been to France two months ago.
7 'I like Mary!' 'Me neither. She's great!'
8 How much biscuits did Ben eat?
9 What did you think of it the film?
10 Steph's really beautiful. She takes up her mother.
11 Tim always shows in front of his friends off.
12 There aren't any milk left for my coffee!
13 Do you want to try in these shoes?
14 Is there any emails for me?
15 In opinion, George is very funny.
16 Harry didn't turn at the party up until midnight.
17 If you ask to me, Sam is a gossip.
18 Did you buy any clothes lately?
19 Lisa's got a little good friends.
20 I made three phone calls since nine o'clock.

Song

1   Read the factfile about the Kinks and answer these questions.

   1   What kind of music did the Kinks play?
   2   What was the original name of the band?
   3   Who were the original members of the band?
   4   Who played the drums after they got their record contract?
   5   What was their first successful song?

factfile

The Kinks were one of the most important British bands in the 1960s and 1970s. They played a mix of traditional pop, country, folk, and blues music and influenced modern bands including Blur and Oasis. Ray and Dave Davies are the most well known members of the band. The brothers were born in London and played the guitar and sang together from an early age. In the early 60s, they formed a band called the Ravens with Peter Quaife as bass guitarist and Micky Willet as drummer. In 1964, they got a record contract with Pye records. They also replaced the drummer with Mick Avory and changed their name to the Kinks. The band's third single, *You really got me* reached the top of the charts in Britain and America. They followed it with famous hits like *Sunny afternoon*, *Waterloo sunset* and *Lola*.

Dedicated follower of fashion

They seek him here, they seek him there,
His clothes are loud, but never square.
It will make or break him so he's got to buy the best,
'cause he's a dedicated follower of fashion.

And when he does his little rounds,
'round the boutiques of London town,
Eagerly pursuing all the latest fads and trends,
'cause he's a dedicated follower of fashion.

Oh yes he is (oh yes he is), oh yes he is (oh yes he is).
There's one thing that he loves and that is flattery.
One week he's in polka-dots, the next week he is in stripes.
'cause he's a dedicated follower of fashion.

They seek him here, they seek him there,
In Regent Street and Leicester Square.
Everywhere the Carnabetian army marches on,
Each one a dedicated follower of fashion.

Oh yes he is (oh yes he is), oh yes he is (oh yes he is).
His world is built 'round discotheques and parties.
This pleasure-seeking individual always looks his best
'cause he's a dedicated follower of fashion.

Oh yes he is (oh yes he is), oh yes he is (oh yes he is).
He flits from shop to shop just like a butterfly.
In matters of the cloth he is as fickle as can be,
'cause he's a dedicated follower of fashion.
He's a dedicated follower of fashion …

2   **32** Listen to the song and choose the correct alternative.

1   What kind of clothes does the man in the song usually buy?
   a   old-fashioned clothes   b   scruffy clothes   c   up-to-date clothes

2   Where does he usually buy them?
   a   in small shops   b   in the biggest stores in London
   c   in different countries around the world

3   In verse 3, what are *polka dots* and *stripes*?
   a   types of material   b   patterns   c   items of clothing

4   Why do you think the singer compares the man to a butterfly in verse 6?
   a   because he wears colourful clothes   b   because he's a weak and fragile person
   c   because he moves quickly from one shop to the next

5   What do you think is the best way to explain the term *dedicated follower of fashion*?
   a   a conservative person
   b   a trendy person
   c   a traditional person

3 Work with a partner and discuss these questions.

1 How important do you think it is to wear fashionable clothes? Why?
2 Do you know anybody who buys new clothes when fashions change? How would you describe them?
3 Do you think fashions change too often? Why can this be a problem?

Speaking: exchanging information

1 Work in groups of three. You are going to a party to meet new people. Follow the instructions.

Step 1: **Prepare new identities**
Make up information about your character. Be as interesting, original and funny as possible. Use the prompts to help you.

Name _____ Age _____
Nationality _____
Marital status (e.g. single / married - how long?
children? / divorced)
_____
Profession (student - subject? / job - how long?)
_____
Taste in films / TV programmes / actors, etc.
_____
Favourite clothes / style, etc. _____
Favourite food _____
Interesting past experiences
(born in another country / have famous parents /
won a competition)

Step 2: **Prepare some questions**
Write questions you would ask someone you meet at a party. Think about personal details, interests, experiences, etc.

Examples:
How many people are there in your family? *What do you think of Jennifer Lopez?*
Have you ever been to Asia?

Step 3: **Practise your conversation**
Practise talking together as a group. Make sure everybody is included in the conversation. Use phrases likes these:
What do you think? *What about you?* *Really? Me too.* *Wow! That's interesting.*

Step 4: **Perform your conversation**

2 Vote to decide which presentation was the funniest.

Extra practice

Unit 1

1 Match the definitions to the phrases.

1 keep a secret ☐

2 have a chat ☐

3 form a bond ☐

4 keep in touch ☐

5 spread rumours ☐

a tell stories that you've heard about other people
b talk about things in an informal way
c stay in contact with somebody
d develop a friendship with somebody
e stay quiet about something you know

2 Complete the survey with the past simple or present perfect simple form of the verbs.

Lately email (1 become) _____ the favourite form of communication for millions of people. Last week we (2 ask) _____ some people what they think ...

'Yesterday, I (3 email) _____ ten friends from work. It's a fantastic and fast way to keep in touch.'
Jane, London

'I (4 not see) _____ my friend, Tom, recently, but we're still in touch by email. It's great!'
Neil, Edinburgh

'I (5 not send) _____ any emails to my ex-friend Katya this year. We (6 have) _____ a bad argument at the end of last year. We (7 not speak) _____ recently and I don't think we will again!'
Sarinder, Liverpool

'Yesterday, my work colleague (8 send) _____ me an email. He sits next to me! I think that's silly!'
Keira, Belfast

3 Write the questions. Use the past simple or present perfect simple form of the verbs.

1 you / spoke / to your best friend / lately?
_____

2 you / send / any emails / yesterday?
_____

3 you / use / your mobile phone / today?
_____

4 you / have a chat / with your parents / recently?
_____

5 you / buy / a new computer / last year?
_____

6 you / see / a good film / this month?
_____

4 Answer the questions in Ex 3 so that they are true for you.

Example:
I spoke to my best friend this morning. She rang me on my mobile.

1 _____
2 _____
3 _____
4 _____
5 _____
6 _____

5 Complete the telephone conversation with the words in the box.

according apparently believe heard
joking really wow

Ivan: Hi, Sarah. It's Ivan.

Sarah: Oh, hi, Ivan. How are things?

Ivan: Listen, you won't (1) _____ this, but Carl's just got married.

Sarah: No! (2) _____? Who to?

Ivan: A girl called Kerry. They only met two months ago.

Sarah: You're (3) _____! I haven't even met her! Where did they get married?

Ivan: (4) _____ to André, they got married in Las Vegas.

Sarah: (5) _____! Are they in Las Vegas now?

Ivan: Yes, but, (6) _____, they're going to Mexico for two weeks.

Sarah: Are they in love, do you think?

Ivan: I (7) _____ that Kerry loves his money!

Sarah: You're a terrible gossip!

Unit 2

1 Answer these questions using the words in the box.

> animation   comedy   historical drama
> martial arts   science fiction   western

Which type of film is …

1   about space or other worlds? _____

2   funny? _____

3   about cowboys usually in America?
_____

4   about karate or kung-fu? _____

5   a cartoon such as *The Simpsons*?
_____

6   usually a serious story about something in the
past? _____

2 Choose the correct alternative.

1   Brad Pitt is *very* / *absolutely* fantastic.

2   Some of the special effects in *Lord of the Rings*
are *really* / *very* spectacular.

3   I didn't like *Police Academy*. It's really *funny* /
childish.

4   The action scenes in Troy are very *impressive* /
brilliant.

5   Johnny Depp is a *pretty* / *absolutely* good actor.

6   Angelina Jolie is *very* / *so* gorgeous.

3 Put the words in italics in the correct order to
complete the dialogue.

A: *do what think of you*
(1) _____ Catherine
Zeta-Jones?

B: *concerned far I'm as as*
(2) _____ she's
gorgeous.

A: *ask if me you* (3) _____
she's not a very good actress.

B: *come oh, on* (4) _____! She
won an Oscar.

A: Well, *my opinion in* (5) _____
she isn't very good.

4 Complete the review with the words in the box.

> background   character   close-ups   played
> scenes   set

TROY is an historical drama and
it's (1) _____ in ancient times. There
are some things I like about it and some
things I don't. I do like the story and the
characters. My favourite (2) _____ in
the film is Achilles, (3) _____ by Brad
Pitt. I especially like the (4) _____ of
Brad's face! He's so handsome! There are
some really good action (5) _____ in
the film, but I don't really like the romance.
It's not very convincing. There are also some
mistakes in the film. For example, Paris and
Helen have a modern umbrella. Also, some
people think the kind of ships we can see in
the (6) _____ weren't used in battle
in those days.

5 Think of a film you have seen recently. Write a
sentence for each heading.

1   title and type of film
_____
_____

2   setting
_____
_____

3   favourite character
_____
_____

4   plot (main story)
_____
_____

5   acting
_____
_____

6   soundtrack and / or special effects
_____
_____

Unit 3

1 Choose the correct alternative.

1 There *isn't / aren't* any biscuits to have with our coffee.

2 There *is / are* some pasta for dinner.

3 There are *a few / a little* tomatoes in the fridge.

4 There aren't *some / any* vegetables in junk food.

5 There *is / are* some meat in this vegetarian pizza!

6 There *isn't / aren't* a lot of salt in this soup.

2 Complete the interview with the words in the box.

> are   few   isn't   little   lot   many   much

Interviewer: Good morning, madam. Can I ask you a (1) _____ questions about your food habits?

Woman: Yes, of course.

Interviewer: How (2) _____ fruit do you eat every week?

Woman: I like fruit. I eat a (3) _____ of apples and bananas.

Interviewer: What about vegetables? How (4) _____ vegetables do you eat every day?

Woman: I like vegetables too. There (5) _____ always vegetables in our house.

Interviewer: Do you prefer butter or margarine?

Woman: I think margarine is healthier, but I sometimes have a (6) _____ butter on my toast.

Interviewer: Do you like sweets and chocolate?

Woman: I love chocolate. That's why there (7) _____ any chocolate in our house!

3 Complete these questions with *How much* or *How many*.

1 _____ Chinese meals do you have every year?

2 _____ meat do you eat in a week?

3 _____ pizzas do you eat in a month?

4 _____ water do you drink every day?

5 _____ biscuits do you usually eat at the weekend?

6 _____ sugar do you add to your coffee?

4 Answer the questions in Ex 3 so that they are true for you. Use *a little, a few, a lot* of or *any*.

Example:

I have a few Chinese meals every year. I like Chinese food.

or

I don't have any Chinese meals. There isn't a Chinese restaurant in our town.

1 _____

2 _____

3 _____

4 _____

5 _____

6 _____

5 Put the words in the correct order to make questions.

1 one, have table Can a please? for I

_____

2 please? menu, could I the see

_____

3 you are order? to ready

_____

4 have some could please? water, I more

_____

5 would any coffee? like you

_____

6 avocado starter? I recommend a Can as

_____

6 Match the questions in Ex 5 to these responses.

a Of course, sir. I'll get one immediately. ☐

b Just the bill, please. ☐

c I'll bring you another bottle. ☐

d I'll just have a main course, thanks. ☐

e Yes, please. I'll just have the fish. ☐

f Certainly, sir. Would you come this way, please? ☐

Unit 4

1 Complete the puzzle with things you wear and words to describe appearance.

1	S			F				
2		T		A				
3		C		S				
4	W			H			
5		S		I			
6			S	O		
7		T		N			
8		G		A		
9				B				
10	N		L		
11		T		E	

Clues
1 It's the opposite of smart.
2 A way of describing typical clothes of your country.
3 Some people think this is a boring way to dress.
4 You use this to tell the time.
5 Women can wear this or trousers.
6 You wear these on your feet.
7 It's another word for fashionable.
8 You wear these for your eyes.
9 It's another word for attractive.
10 It's an item of jewellery.
11 Men often wear one when they go to work.

2 Describe these people. Use the words in Ex 1 and the words in the box to help you.

| accessories | casual | earring | smart |
| up-to-date | trousers |

Example:
The woman is scruffy. She's wearing old trousers and socks. She isn't wearing any accessories.

1 _____
_____
_____
_____
_____

2 _____
_____
_____
_____
_____
_____

3 _____
_____
_____
_____
_____

3 Correct the mistake in these sentences.
Example: *it*
Nobody can come to the party so we're calling ∧ off.

1 I didn't like the earrings, so I gave away them.

2 The fire alarm went it off during the fashion show.

3 I came across them some old magazines when I was tidying my bedroom.

4 I went to a beauty salon and they made it up my face. I looked great.

5 I can't come to the party because I have to look her after my sister.

4 Complete the note with the correct form of the phrasal verbs in the boxes.

Hi Hannah

| show off | put on | dress up |

How are you? Can I ask you a big favour? Have you got any clothes I can borrow? I'm going to a work party in a posh hotel and I need to wear something smart. You know how people always (1) _____ for these things! They always (2) _____ their most expensive clothes and (3) _____ to everyone!

| get up | take after | try on |

I tried to get something this morning, but I didn't do very well. I (4) _____ early and went into town. I (5) _____ a lot of clothes, but I didn't buy anything. I think I (6) _____ my mum. She never buys anything either.

| come across | turn up |

Anyway, when I was going home, I (7) _____ a fantastic Italian restaurant. We must go there when we've got some money! Hope you have something I can wear! I can't (8) _____ looking scruffy!

Love
Mel

Grammar reference

Unit 1

Talking about recent events

For past events in a finished time period, you use the past simple. For past events in an unfinished time period, you use the present perfect.

Past simple

You use the past simple form of the verb.
*She **phoned** last night.*
*He **went** home at 10 pm.*

Words and phrases like *last year*, *yesterday*, etc. tell us that the event started and finished in the past – a finished time period.
*She **took** her final exams **last year**.*
*I **saw** Fiona **yesterday**.*

You <u>can</u> use the past simple with words and phrases like *this month*, t*oday*, *this week*, etc., but only when you are referring to something that happened in a finished time period.
*I **went** shopping **today**.* (Perhaps *this morning* or *this afternoon* – now it is clearly later and the time period referred to is finished.)

ago

You use *ago* with the past simple to talk about how long before now something happened.
*He **moved** here two years **ago**.* (He moved here two years before now.)

Present perfect simple

> has /have ('s / 've) + past participle

*She's **phoned** three times today.*
*Simon or Emma? Sorry they've **gone** home.*

Words and phrases like *this month*, *recently*, etc. tell us that we are still in the time referred to. The time period is unfinished.
*I've **seen** three films at the cinema **this month**.*
*They **haven't called** us **recently**.*

You <u>can't</u> use the present perfect to talk about things which happened in a finished time period.
~~I've been shopping yesterday.~~
*I **went** shopping **yesterday**.*

Unit 2

Asking for and giving opinions

There are many ways of asking for and giving opinions. This is probably the most common way of asking for an opinion:
***What do you think** of Australian wine?*

When someone asks for your opinion, you can just give it.
A: *What do you think of my hat?*   **B:** *It's lovely.*

However, it is more usual to signal that you are going to give an opinion by using one of a number of set phrases.
***I think** it's the best in the world.*
***In my opinion**, French wine is still the best.*
***If you ask me**, South African wine is better.*
***As far as I'm concerned**, New Zealand makes much better wine.*

There are several ways to agree with an opinion.
Me too. | Me neither.
Same here.

There are also several ways to disagree with an opinion.
Really?
Oh, come on.

Unit 3

Quantifiers with countable and uncountable nouns

Used with countable nouns
many and *a lot (of)*

You use *many* to talk about countable nouns. It is used mainly in questions and negative sentences. Look out for the plural *s* on the end of the noun (except for irregular nouns, like *people*).
A: *How **many** shops have you been to today?*
B: *Not **many**.Why?*
A: *Are there **many** people there?*   **B:** *No, not many.*

It is formal to use *many* in positive sentences. It is more common to use *a lot (of)*.
*I wrote **a lot of** e-mails on Friday. I received **a lot**, too.*

a few

A few means 'a small quantity' and is used only with countable nouns.
*There are only **a few** restaurants in the town.*
A: *Were there many people there?*   **B:** *A few.*

Used with uncountable nouns
much and *a lot (of)*

You use *much* to talk about uncountable nouns. It is used mainly in questions and negative sentences. Uncountable nouns only appear in singular form, so do not have the plural *s* at the end.

A: *Is there **much** milk left?*   B: *No, not **much**.*
A: *How **much** time did you spend there?*   B: *Not **much**.*

It is unusual to use *much* in positive sentences. It is more common to use *a lot (of)*.
*There's **a lot of** cream.*
*How much time? Quite **a lot**, actually.*

a little

A little means 'a small quantity' and is used only with uncountable nouns.
A: *How much sugar is there?*   B: *A little.*

Used with countable and uncountable nouns

Some and *any* can both be used with countable and uncountable nouns. They are both frequently used with *-one*, *-body*, *-thing* and *-where* (*someone*, *anyone*, etc.).

some

You use *some* in questions if you expect the answer to be 'yes'.
*You look thirsty. Would you like **some** water?*

You use *some* to talk about a limited quantity of something (or things).
*There are **some** plates in the cupboard.*
*There is **some** cake in the fridge.*

You can't use *some* in negative statements.
~~*There isn't some cake in the fridge.*~~

any

You use *any* in questions to ask about an unlimited or unspecified quantity.
*Is there **any** mail?*
*Are there **any** eggs left?*

You use *any* in negative statements.
*There isn't **any** mail.*
*No, there aren't **any** eggs left.*

Unit 4
Recognising and using phrasal verbs

When you find phrasal verbs in a text, there are four simple steps you should follow to help you understand them. Once you have identified the phrasal verb (usually a simple verb like *turn*, *go*, *come*, etc. followed by one or two particles, like *up*, *down*, *out*, etc.) follow these steps:

Recognising phrasal verbs

Step 1

Try to guess the meaning of the phrasal verb from its context.
*As usual, my alarm **went off** at six thirty this morning.*
The context of *six thirty this morning* and *alarm* may help you to guess that *went off* means rang or started making a noise.

Step 2

Check your guess in a dictionary. Search for the meaning you expect because some phrasal verbs have more than one meaning. *Go off* has several other meanings.

Using phrasal verbs

If you want to use a phrasal verb, you need to know if the verb needs an object, or not. Your dictionary will give you this information. If it needs an object, it is called a *transitive* verb (or T). If it doesn't need an object, it is called an *intransitive* verb (or I).

Step 3

Check if the phrasal verb is transitive or intransitive. The use of *go off* that we are using is intransitive, so we know everything about the verb that we need to know.
*The alarm **went off** at 6.30 am.*
However, if the verb needs an object, you need to go to the final stage, Step 4.

Step 4

If the phrasal verb needs an object, it is transitive. There are two types of transitive phrasal verb:

1   Separable (i.e. it can be separated)
    The object can go between or after the two parts of the verb.
    *He **tried** the jacket **on**.*
    *He **tried on** the jacket.*

With separable verbs, if you want to use a pronoun (*it*, *him*, *her*, *them*, etc.) you must put it between the two parts of the verb.
*He **tried** it **on**.*

2   Non-separable (i.e. it can't be separated)
    The object must always go after the verb, even if it's a pronoun.
    *He **takes after** his father.*
    *He **takes after** him.*

Wordlist

*** the 2,500 most common English words, ** very common words, * fairly common words

Unit 1

according to *prep* /ə'kɔ:dɪŋ ,tu:, tə/ ***
apparently *adv* /ə'pærəntli/ ***
cheap *adj* /tʃi:p/ ***
communication skills *n pl* /kə,mju:nɪ'keɪʃn ,skɪlz/ ***
ex *n* /eks/
expensive *adj* /ɪk'spensɪv/ ***
face to face *adv* /,feɪs tə 'feɪs/
form a bond *v* /,fɔ:m ə 'bɒnd/ **
friendship *n* /'frendʃɪp/ **
gossip *v, n* /'gɒsɪp/
Guess what? *phrase* /,ges 'wɒt/
half *det* /hɑ:f/ ***
have a baby *v* /,hæv ə 'beɪbi/ ***
have a chat *v* /,hæv ə 'tʃæt/ *
Have you heard? *phrase* /,hæv ju: 'hɜ:d/
I heard that ... *phrase* /aɪ ,hɜ:d ðət/
keep a secret *phrase* /,ki:p ə 'si:krət/
keep in touch *phrase* /,ki:p ɪn 'tʌtʃ/
last week *phrase* /,lɑ:st 'wi:k/
No! Really? *phrase* /,nəʊ 'rɪəli/
number one *adj* /,nʌmbə 'wʌn/
put on weight *phrase* /,pʊt ɒn 'weɪt/
a quarter *det* /ə 'kwɔ:tə/ ***
recently *adv* /'ri:səntli/ ***
share *v* /ʃeə/ ***
split up with *v* /,splɪt 'ʌp wɪð/ **
spread rumours *v* /,spred 'ru:məz/ **
a third *det* /ə 'θɜ:d/
today *n* /tə'deɪ/ ***
Wow! *phrase* /waʊ/
yesterday *n* /'jestədeɪ/ ***
You won't believe this! *phrase* /ju: ,wəʊnt bɪ'li:v ðɪs/
You're joking! *phrase* /jɔ: 'dʒəʊkɪŋ/

Unit 2

absolutely *adj* /'æbsə'lu:tli/ ***
action scenes *n pl* /'ækʃn ,si:nz/ ***
animation *n* /,ænɪ'meɪʃn/
As far as I'm concerned *phrase* /əz ,fɑ:r əz 'aɪm kən,sɜ:nd/
aviator *n* /'eɪvi,eɪtə/
biography *n* /baɪ'ɒgrəfi/ *
brilliant *adj* /'brɪliənt/ ***
business *n* /'bɪznəs/ ***
character *n* /'kærɪktə/ ***
childish *adj* /'tʃaɪldɪʃ/ *
close-up *n* /'kləʊs ʌp/
comedy *n* /'kɒmədi/ **
convincingly *adv* /kən'vɪnsɪŋli/
corruption *n* /kə'rʌpʃn/ **
devote *v* /dɪ'vəʊt/
fantasy *n* /'fæntəsi/ **
gangster movie *n* /'gæŋstə ,mu:vi/
gorgeous *adj* /'gɔ:dʒəs/ *
government *n* /'gʌvnmənt/ ***
hesitation *n* /,hezɪ'teɪʃn/ *
historical drama *n* /hɪ,stɒrɪkl 'drɑ:mə/ ***
horror *n* /'hɒrə/ **
I think ... *phrase* /,aɪ 'θɪŋk/
If you ask me, ... *phrase* /ɪf ju: ,ɑ:sk 'mi:/
impressive *adj* /ɪm'presɪv/ **
In my opinion *phrase* /ɪn ,maɪ ə,pɪnjən/
in the background *phrase* /,ɪn ðə 'bækgraʊnd/
martial arts *n pl* /,mɑ:ʃl 'ɑ:ts/ *
Me too *phrase* /,mi: 'tu:/
Oh, come on! *phrase* /,əʊ ,kʌm 'ɒn/
play (played by) *v* /pleɪ ('pleɪd baɪ)/ ***
pretty *adj* /'prɪti/ ***
property *n* /'prɒpəti/ ***
really *adv* /'rɪəli/ ***
recluse *n* /rɪ'klu:s/
role *n* /rəʊl/ ***
romance *n* /rəʊ'mæns/ *

Unit 3

Same here *phrase* /,seɪm 'hɪə/
scene *n* /si:n/ ***
science fiction *n* /,saɪəns 'fɪkʃn/ *
set *v* /set/ ***
so *adv* /səʊ/ ***
soundtrack *n* /'saʊndtræk/
special effects *n pl* /,speʃl ɪ'fekts/
spectacular *adj* /spek'tækjələ/ **
very *adv* /'veri/ ***
war drama *n* /'wɔ: ,drɑ:mə/ ***
western *n* /'westən/
What did you think of it? *phrase* /,wɒt dɪd ju: ,θɪŋk əv ɪt/

Unit 3

barbecue *n* /'bɑ:bɪ,kju:/ *
biscuit *n* /'bɪskɪt/ **
book *v* /bʊk/ **
bottle *n* /'bɒtl/ ***
bowl *n* /bəʊl/ **
butter *n* /'bʌtə/ **
carrot *n* /'kærət/ *
change *n* /tʃeɪndʒ/ ***
chicken *n* /'tʃɪkɪn/ **
chopsticks *n pl* /'tʃɒpstɪks/
company *n* /'kʌmpəni/ ***
courgette *n* /kɔ:'ʒet/
cream *n* /kri:m/ **
customary *adj* /'kʌstəməri/ *
dessert *n* /dɪ'zɜ:t/ *
egg *n* /eg/ ***
flour *n* /'flaʊə/ *
fork *n* /fɔ:k/ **
formal *adj* /'fɔ:ml/ ***
glass *n* /glɑ:s/ ***
green beans *n pl* /,gri:n 'bi:nz/
informally *adv* /ɪn'fɔ:məli/
knife *n* /naɪf/ ***
lettuce *n* /'letɪs/ *
main course *n* /,meɪn 'kɔ:s/
margarine *n* /,mɑ:dʒə'ri:n/
mask *n* /mɑ:sk/ *
meat *n* /mi:t/ ***
mushrooms *n pl* /'mʌʃru:mz/ *
naturally *adv* /'nætʃrəli/ ***
noodles *n pl* /'nu:dlz/
offend *v* /ə'fend/ *
olive oil *n* /,ɒlɪv 'ɔɪl/
onions *n pl* /'ʌnjənz/ **
order *v* /'ɔ:də/ ***
pepper *n* /'pepə/ *
plate *n* /pleɪt/ ***
politely *adv* /pə'laɪtli/ *
potato *n* /pə'teɪtəʊ/ **
put sb off (sthg) *v* /,pʊt ... 'ɒf .../
recommend *v* /,rekə'mend/ ***
rice *n* /raɪs/ **
salt *n* /sɔ:lt/ **
spaghetti *n* /spə'geti/
spoon *n* /spu:n/ **
starter *n* /'stɑ:tə/ *
steak *n* /steɪk/ *
sugar *n* /'ʃʊgə/ ***
taste *n* /teɪst/ ***
thirsty *adj* /'θɜ:sti/ *
tip *n* /tɪp/ **
tomato *n* /tə'mɑ:təʊ/ **
vanilla *n* /və'nɪlə/
vegetables *n pl* /'vedʒtəblz/ ***
vinegar *n* /'vɪnɪgə/
wine *n* /waɪn/ ***

Unit 4

accessories *n pl* /ək'sesəriz/ **
attractive *adj* /ə'træktɪv/ ***
beautiful *adj* /'bju:tɪfl/ ***
beauty contest *n* /'bju:ti ,kɒntest/
call off *v* /,kɔ:l 'ɒf/
casual *adj* /'kæʒuəl/ **
charm *n* /tʃɑ:m/ **
come across *v* /'kʌm ə,krɒs/
conservative *adj* /kən'sɜ:vətɪv/ **
criminal *n* /'krɪmɪnl/ **
dress up *v* /,dres 'ʌp/
earrings *n pl* /'ɪərɪŋz/ *
fashionable *adj* /'fæʃnəbl/ **
get up *v* /,get 'ʌp/
give away *v* /,gɪv ə'weɪ/
glasses *n pl* /'glɑ:sɪz/ *
go off *v* /,gəʊ 'ɒf/
good-looking *adj* /,gʊd 'lʊkɪŋ/ **
hairstyle *n* /'heəstaɪl/ *
henna *n* /'henə/
look after *v* /,lʊk 'ɑ:ftə/
looks *n pl* /lʊks/ ***
make up *v* /,meɪk 'ʌp/
mohican *n* /məʊ'hi:kən/
necklace *n* /'nekləs/ *
old-fashioned *adj* /,əʊld 'fæʃnd/ **
personality *n* /,pɜ:sə'næləti/ ***
piercing *n* /'pɪəsɪŋ/
powder *n* /'paʊdə/ **
put on *v* /,pʊt 'ɒn/
scruffy *adj* /'skrʌfi/
show off *v* /,ʃəʊ 'ɒf/
skirt *n* /skɜ:t/ **
smart *adj* /smɑ:t/ **
smile *n* /smaɪl/ ***
socks *n pl* /sɒks/ *
style *n* /staɪl/ ***
take after *v* /,teɪk 'ɑ:ftə/
tattoo *n* /tæ'tu:/
tie *n* /taɪ/ **
traditional *adj* /trə'dɪʃn(ə)l/ ***
trendy *adj* /'trendi/
trousers *n* /'traʊzəz/ **
try on *v* /,traɪ 'ɒn/
turn up *v* /,tɜ:n 'ʌp/
up-to-date *adj* /ʌp tə 'deɪt/ *
watch *n* /wɒtʃ/ **

Communication activities

Unit 2, Language study Ex 5 page 40

1 Read the statements and decide how you feel about each one.

What do you think?

Mark each statement 1–5 to show how you feel.

> 1 = strongly agree   4 = generally disagree
> 2 = generally agree   5 = strongly disagree
> 3 = not sure

a Political leaders should stay in power for a maximum of three years only. ☐

b There is never any good reason for using weapons. ☐

c Murderers should be kept in prison for the rest of their lives. ☐

d Marriage isn't really important or relevant in today's world. ☐

e Children are maturing earlier, so the right to vote should be lowered to 14. ☐

f Smoking should be banned in all indoor public places. ☐

g Children under the age of three shouldn't be allowed to watch TV. ☐

h Religious teaching, and clothing, should be kept out of all schools. ☐

i Professional footballers are paid too much. ☐

j If children under the age of 16 break the law, their parents should be punished. ☐

2 Work in groups and discuss your ideas. Use the words and phrases in the box to help you.

> As far as I'm concerned …   If you ask me …   In my opinion …   I think …
> Me too.   Oh, come on.   Really?   Same here.   What do you think about this?

Unit 3, Language study Ex 7 page 43

Student A

1 You are going to cook a meal for some friends. Look at the recipe and call your flatmate (Student B) and check if you have all the ingredients you need in the house.

Examples:
Is there any (milk)?   *Are there any (mushrooms)?*
How much?   *How many?*

2 Make a shopping list of everything that you need to buy. Read your shopping list to Student B.

Recipe

Chicken Doria
chicken, mushrooms, onions, butter,
white wine, flour, cream, cheese

Salad
lettuce, tomatoes, olive oil,
vinegar, salt, pepper

Dessert (crème caramel)
sugar, eggs (6), milk, vanilla

Fruit
apples, oranges

Listening scripts

Unit 1 Don't breathe a word!

 Listening script 17

Reading text from page 35

 Listening script 18

Conversation 1
(J = Justin, N = Nick)
J: Hi, Nick.
N: Have you heard?
J: Heard what?
N: About Mika.
J: No. What?
N: According to Roger, she's gone crazy. Apparently, she left her job yesterday and now she wants to go to Thailand and live on a beach.
J: Wow! Why do you think she's done that?
N: It may be something to do with Ben. You know? Her ex-boyfriend. Well, he split up with his new girlfriend last week. I heard that he wants to go to Asia to sell jewellery.
J: Well, that's it then, isn't it? I'm sure you're right. So I guess she's still in love with him then …

Conversation 2
(A = Ashley, L = Lisa)
A: Hi, Lisa.
L: Ash! Guess what!
A: What?
L: Sara's had her baby!
A: No! Really? When?
L: Today. This morning. She's still in the hospital with her husband and Marco.
A: Her brother Marco?
L: Yeah, and you won't believe this!
A: What? Tell me, tell me.
L: He's put on so much weight.
A: You're joking! It must have happened recently because I saw him three months ago and he looked great.
L: Yes. Oh, he's still good looking, he's just … well, bigger.

Unit 2 Pass the popcorn, please

 Listening script 19

Reading text from page 39

 Listening script 20

(J = Jack, C = Chloe, R = Ralph)
J: Well? What did you think of it?
C: I thought it was absolutely fantastic!
J: Yeah, me too.
C: Johnny Depp is so funny and so gorgeous, and he makes a great pirate.
J: How about you, Ralph? What did you think of it?
R: In my opinion, it was really childish, not very funny and it went on too long.
J: Really? What did you think about the action scenes? They were pretty impressive, weren't they?
C: Yes, I thought they were absolutely brilliant, too! And the special effects were really spectacular.
R: OK, the special effects were pretty good, but I noticed some historical mistakes. As far as I'm concerned, Hollywood doesn't care enough about historical accuracy – exploding shells didn't exist in the 1600s …

C: Oh, come on, Ralph. Don't you think you're taking it all a bit too seriously? It's supposed to be a comedy.
R: Maybe, but I'm still going to post a message on the Movie Mistakes page so that other people can see the mistake too.
J: Post a message? If you ask me, the people who read those messages are worse than the people who make the mistakes.
C: Same here. Ralph, I think you need to get yourself a girlfriend.

 Listening script 21

1   absolutely fantastic
2   so funny
3   so gorgeous
4   really childish
5   not very funny
6   pretty impressive
7   absolutely brilliant
8   really spectacular
9   pretty good

 Listening script 22

A: What do you think of Leonardo DiCaprio?
B: I think he's gorgeous.
C: Me too.
A: Really? If you ask me, Johnny Depp is more interesting.
C: Ooh, same here. I prefer him, actually.
B: Oh, come on! Johnny Depp's too old now.
A: As far as I'm concerned, they both are.

 Listening script 23

A: What do you think of Hollywood movies?
B: In my opinion, they're boring.
A: Really? I think they're fantastic.
B: If you ask me, Spanish films are much better.
A: Oh, come on! You see the same actors in every film.
B: True, but the acting is really great.

Unit 3 You must try it

 Listening script 24

Reading text from page 42

 Listening script 25

Vocabulary Ex 1 from page 44

 Listening script 26

A: I'd like a table for one, please.
B: Certainly, sir. Have you booked?
A: No, I haven't.
B: No problem. Would you come this way, please?
A: Could I see the menu, please?
B: Of course, sir. I'll get you one immediately.
B: Are you ready to order?
A: Yes, please.
B: Any starters?
A: I'll just have the spaghetti, please.
B: Main course. Certainly. Anything else?
A: No, thanks. Oh, excuse me, could I have some more water, please?
B: I'll bring you another bottle, sir.
B: Would you like any dessert, or coffee?
A: Just the bill, please.
B: Certainly. That'll be £12.50, please.
A: Here you are. Thanks.
B: Thank you very much, sir. See you again, I hope. What a lovely man and what a generous tip.

 Listening script 27

A lot of people worry about doing the wrong thing when they eat in another country. My advice is: don't worry. Most of the time, the rules are the same around the world: don't put your elbows on the table, don't speak with your mouth full. That sort of thing. But sometimes it helps if you know one or two things about the place where you are eating. I was at a formal dinner in Canada with a friend who saw all the knives and forks and said, 'What do I do? How do I know which ones to use?' She was so worried, but I told her, 'Just start on the outside and work in.' Easy. It's the same all over the world, where people use a knife and fork.

But you have to be careful if you're in a country where they use chopsticks. I was enjoying a delicious meal in China and I wanted to put my chopsticks down for a moment. I didn't want to put them on the table – it seemed dirty – so I stuck them into my bowl of rice. Two or three people quickly told me that this was bad manners and so I rested them across my plate, and that was OK. That was a cultural mistake, but sometimes the mistake may offend someone's religious beliefs. In Tunisia, which is a Muslim country, I picked up a piece of bread in my left hand. My Tunisian friend told me that I should use my right hand to pick up food. It is bad manners to use the left hand to pick up food or shake someone's hand. I think that is important to know.

Traditions, though, are not always so important. In Britain people argue about how to make tea properly – do you put the milk in first or the tea in first? The truth is, it's not really important. You won't offend anyone if you get the order wrong. You might offend a lot of people, though, if you drink your tea loudly. Slurping your food or drink is not generally regarded as polite behaviour. It's the same in Asia, but there is an exception. It's perfectly acceptable to make a noise when eating noodles, particularly if you are a man. I was at a noodle restaurant in Japan, with a friend, a young Japanese man, and he told me that if I make a lot of noise eating my noodles, the chef will be happy. Of course I tried, but I have to say it felt strange.

If you're invited to someone's house for a meal, it's common across Europe to take a bottle of wine, or flowers. It's the same in Australia, where I'm from, but if you are invited to a barbecue at someone's house, it's really important to relax and show that you are enjoying yourself. We usually dress casually for a barbecue and treat it as a very informal occasion. You shouldn't be too formal – don't wait for service, serve yourself. It shows the host that you really feel at home. They will feel relaxed if they see that you are relaxed.

Unit 4 Followers of fashion

 Listening script 28

Reading text from page 46

 Listening script 29

(E = Ellen, F = Frank)

E: Is tattooing an old custom?

F: Oh yeah, tattoos have been around for a long time. The Greeks and the Egyptians had tattoos, and that was in about 2,000 BC. Some people have found examples of tattoos from as far back as 3,500 BC.

E: Wow! That's over 5,000 years ago. So, where does the word tattoo come from?

F: It comes from the Tahitian word 'tatau', which means 'to mark'. When the explorer Captain Cook sailed to the South Pacific – you know Captain Cook?

E: Sure. The man that discovered Australia in the 1800s.

F: It was in 1770, actually, but that's not really important. Anyway, he saw lots of people in the Pacific islands wearing tattoos, and when he saw the Maoris …

E: In New Zealand? The Maoris of New Zealand?

F: Exactly. When he saw the Maoris, he was really impressed. The old men's faces and bodies were covered in tattoos. Now, of course, the Maori-style tattoo is famous, and fashionable, all over the world. By the way, is that OK? Does it hurt?

E: No, it's fine, thanks. So, have people always tattooed themselves just to look good?

F: Most of the time, yeah, but in some cultures tattoos tell us about the person's position in society. For example, the early Romans tattooed criminals. In Tahiti, your tattoos tell the story of your life. And a long time ago, sailors travelling to exotic countries collected tattoos as souvenirs – a famous symbol of China is the dragon, so when sailors went to China they usually had a tattoo of a dragon to show where they had been. People still like having dragon tattoos because they're so beautiful, not because they've been to China.

E: These days I guess people get tattooed because it's trendy, don't they?

F: In this country, yes. Young people who want to stay up-to-date have a tattoo, but it's not the same in every country. In Japan, having a lot of tattoos is often a sign that you are a member of the yakuza, the Japanese mafia.

E: Really? So, I shouldn't go to Japan with this, then?

F: This is a small tattoo – not a big problem. These days, more and more fashionable young Japanese are getting a small tattoo. The yakuza are covered in beautiful tattoos, on their back and their front, so don't worry, you need a lot more work than this. Out of interest, why did you choose to have this particular tattoo?

E: Oh, because everyone in the world understands what it is – it's not a pretty picture, it's a code. You see it on everything that you buy. I think it's really modern, and my favourite singer has one exactly the same.

 Listening script 30

(E = Ellen, F = Frank)

F: Your favourite singer? Which singer has a tattoo of a bar code?

E: Pink. She's got it on the back of her neck.

F: On her neck, eh? I suppose it's better than the one David Beckham's got on his neck – it's a cross, with wings.

E: Mm, it's too big. I prefer the smaller ones like the little bird Johnny Depp's got on his arm …

F: Mm, I must say, I like the bigger tattoos. The singer Robbie Williams has got a large Maori design on his arm and Angelina Jolie has got a really large, beautiful tiger on her back. That must have taken a long time to do …

Unit 5 Review

 Listening script 31

(M = Maya, H = Hannah, J = Josh)

M: I read an interesting article about taste this morning.

H: Oh, yeah?

M: Yeah. It talks about how people like each other because they have the same tastes. What do you think of that, Josh?

J: I disagree. I think some people like each other and they've got completely different tastes. Take this old friend of mine, Miguel. We're completely different. He's noisy and likes football and martial arts. I'm quiet and I prefer reading and going to the cinema. My idea of a good night out is watching a good comedy film. Miguel would hate that.

M: So why do you like him, then?

J: I think, well, when we met, we didn't know anybody at college and, you know, I think we just formed a strong bond early on. It didn't matter that we didn't have the same tastes in anything.

H: Did you study the same subjects?

J: No. He did computer studies and I did film studies.

M: Do you keep in touch?

J: Yeah. I saw him last week and we usually have a chat on the phone about two or three times a week.

M: What about you, Hannah?

H: I agree with Josh. I like Grace, my manager at work, but we've got completely different tastes. For a start, Grace wears up-to-date clothes and I mean really up-to-date. She spends loads of money on fashion and she looks absolutely fantastic.

M: You look good too, Hannah.

H: Oh, come on! I wear scruffy jeans all the time. But, thanks. Oh, and we've got different ideas about food, too.

M: Food?

H: Yeah, Grace is really healthy. At lunchtime, she eats lots of fruit and vegetables. She never eats fast food. She hates the stuff.

M: Really? She sounds great. I think good food is important too.

H: Yes, well, I agree with you, Maya, but I also love hamburgers and chips. Anyway, it doesn't matter that we don't have the same taste in fashion, or in food, she's a great manager and I like her.

J: Hmm. What about you, Maya? What do you think?

M: As far as I'm concerned, the most important quality in a person is that you can trust them. I mean, I phone my best friend almost every day and tell her my news – you know, personal stuff, and it's really important for me to feel that she can keep a secret.

J: Yeah, I suppose so. But sometimes I like talking to people who can't keep a secret! A little bit of gossip can be really interesting.

H: Well, if you like gossip – only the other day, I saw Howard and he told me …

 Listening script 32

Song from page 52

Communication activities

Unit 3, Language study Ex 7 page 43

Student B

1   Your flatmate (Student A) wants you to check the fridge and shelves for some items. Listen to your flatmate and answer his / her questions.

Examples:
Yes, there are (some / a lot / a few).   Yes, there is (some / a lot / a little).   No, there aren't any.   No, there isn't any.

2   When you've finished checking the fridge and shelves, Student A will read a shopping list to you. Check that all of these items are on Student A's shopping list: mushrooms, cheese, lettuce, tomatoes, olive oil, eggs, vanilla and oranges.

Unit 4, Listening and speaking Ex 4 page 49

▲ Angelina Jolie   ▲ Pink   ▲ David Beckham   ▲ Johnny Depp   ▲ Robbie Williams

Module 3
Motion

Unit	Topic	Language study	Vocabulary	Main skills
1 **Get down to the rhythm** pages 66–69	• Shake that thing (types and origins of music) • It's party time (festivals)	• *for* and *since* with the present perfect	• Types of music • Musical instruments	• **Reading:** ordering a text summary • **Speaking:** talking about music and festivals • **Pronunciation:** recognising strong and weak forms in sentences • **Listening:** identifying main information
2 **Just do it** pages 70–73	• Hit the streets (an unusual new sport: parkour) • Get moving (skating into work)	• Comparatives and superlatives	• *play, do, go* with sports and activities • Phrases with *get*	• **Listening:** understanding gist and identifying key information • **Speaking:** discussing sport and exercise • **Reading:** selecting an appropriate title • **Writing:** a short story with sequencers
3 **On the road again** pages 74–77	• Save our soles (three pilgrimage experiences) • Take a break (holidays)	• *say* and *tell* • Direct and indirect speech	• Prepositions of place • Words to describe location, accommodation and holiday activities	• **Reading:** understanding key details and summarising a story • **Listening:** identifying main information • **Speaking:** Discussing travel and holiday preferences
4 **Out and about** pages 78–81	• Trouble in store (making complaints in shops) • What do I say? (shopping quiz)	• Talking about real and imaginary situations (first and second conditionals)	• Shopping vocabulary	• **Listening:** Understanding mood and manner • **Reading:** understanding gist • **Writing:** a short dialogue • **Speaking:** buying and returning goods

5 **Review unit** pages 82–85
• **Extra practice** pages 86–89 • **Grammar reference and wordlist** pages 90–92 • **Listening scripts:** pages 94–95 • **Communication activities:** pages 93, 96
• **Use CD2 for listening activities in this module.**

1 Get down to the rhythm

LEARNING AIMS

- Can use *for* and *since* with the present perfect
- Can recognise strong and weak forms in sentences
- Can talk about music and festivals

Shake that thing

Lead-in 1 Work in groups and discuss what type of music you listen to when you:

1	are working	3	feel happy	5	want to relax
2	feel sad	4	are travelling		

2 **01** Listen to these nine pieces of music. How many can you match to the styles in the box?

> Bhangra   Blues   Calypso   Classical   Fado   Han   Jazz   Samba
> Zulu (Mbube)

3 Which places do you associate each style with? Check your ideas on page 93.

4 Work with a partner and discuss these questions.

1 What kind of music is popular in your country among the young, the middle-aged and the elderly?
2 What kind of music is your country famous for?
3 What type of music is played at festivals in your country?

Reading 1 **02** Read the article on page 67 and explain the connection between these things.

1	carnival and Easter	3	samba and West Africa
2	jazz and New Orleans	4	steel drums and Trinidad

2 Read the text again and answer these questions.

1 Which countries took carnival to the Americas?
2 What is the name of the festival that takes place in New Orleans?
3 The Brazilian dance *maxixe* is a mixture of musical styles from which two other places?
4 What styles of music can you expect to hear at the Trinidad carnival?

3 Match the words to the prepositions. Then find the word combinations in the text.

1	arrive	for
2	come	from
3	famous	in
4	mix	of
5	think	with

4 Put this summary of the text in the correct order. Use the word combinations in Ex 3 to help you.

a   in the Americas, they took the music of their roots and mixed it ☐

b   of New Orleans when we hear jazz. These are just some of the ☐

c   Many of the musical styles we listen to these days actually come ☐ 1

d   from mixing the music of two cultures. When Africans arrived ☐

e   for samba music and Trinidad for calypso, and we usually think ☐

f   with European music. And the result? Brazil is now famous ☐

g   styles that combine African and European rhythms. ☐

Carnival roots

People around the world have celebrated carnival for thousands of years. In Europe, carnival was usually held about six weeks before Easter. It was the last opportunity for Christians to eat, drink and enjoy themselves before the long period of fasting leading up to Easter. This tradition was taken to the American colonies by the French, Spanish and Portuguese. In America, it changed as it came into contact with other traditions, mainly from the African slaves that were brought across the Atlantic.

Life for the African slaves in the sugar and cotton plantations was hard. There were very few occasions to celebrate. When they did celebrate, they displayed great energy in dance and music.

Over the years, the celebrations have developed in different ways, depending on the city or country. In the United States, New Orleans is famous for its brass band sound, particularly during the Mardi Gras festival. New Orleans mixed blues (sad songs) with trumpets and trombones, and made a new type of music: jazz. People have been playing jazz since the early 20th century.

The Portuguese took their folk music to Brazil when they arrived in South America in 1500. Over time, this guitar, violin and accordion music mixed with the faster tempo of African rhythms. This produced upbeat dances like the happy and optimistic maxixe. The world famous carnival in Rio de Janeiro moves to the beat of samba. We think of Brazil when we hear samba, but the origins of samba lie in West Africa.

Trinidad, the Caribbean island that has exported carnival to so many countries, is famous for calypso. It comes from kalinda music, originally from Africa. The steel drums, played at every Trinidad carnival, were originally the lids of dustbins. Now carnival has all types of music from hip-hop, house and salsa as well as the more traditional sounds of calypso.

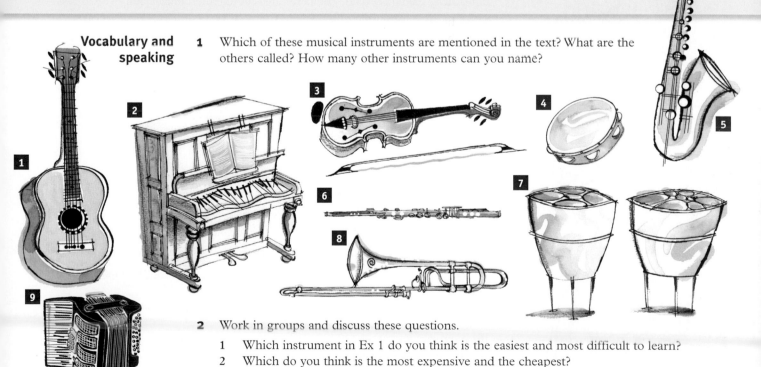

Vocabulary and speaking

1 Which of these musical instruments are mentioned in the text? What are the others called? How many other instruments can you name?

2 Work in groups and discuss these questions.

1 Which instrument in Ex 1 do you think is the easiest and most difficult to learn?
2 Which do you think is the most expensive and the cheapest?
3 Do you play an instrument? Which would you like to play well?
4 Can you think of a piece of music which sounds happy or sad because of the instrument that plays it?
5 What are the traditional or special instruments played in your country? Do you like the sound they make?

LANGUAGE STUDY

for and *since* with the present perfect

1   Look at these sentences from the article on page 67. Which word do we use to talk about:
a   a point in time?   b   a period of time?

*People around the world have celebrated carnival **for** thousands of years.*
*People have been playing jazz **since** the early 20th century.*

2   Which tense is used in the two example sentences in Ex 1?

Grammar reference page 90

For	Since
a few minutes	I was born

3   Put the phrases in the box in the correct list.

> ~~a few minutes~~   ~~I was born~~   ages   a long time   I was young   last week
> three o'clock   25 years   two months   2005

4   Complete these lines from songs with *for* or *since*.
1   We've known each other _____ we were young.
2   I've loved you _____ the first time I saw you.
3   I've been looking for someone like you _____ such a long time.
4   You've been on my mind _____ yesterday.
5   I've thought of nothing but you _____ two months.

5   Look at the path of Howlin' Hopkins' life. Complete his biography with either a point in time (e.g. *1999*) or a period of time (e.g. *ten years*) up to now.

Howlin' Hopkins was just a small boy when he started playing the saxophone. He loved playing it and everyone loved listening to him play. When he was older, he moved to Chicago and, soon afterwards, he joined a blues band called So Blue. The band are still together and he still lives in Chicago. He's lived there for (1) _____ years and he's been in So Blue since (2) _____. He plays other instruments but his favourite is the saxophone. He's been playing since (3) _____ and he doesn't think he'll ever stop. His life isn't all the same, though. He's married now, to his long time girlfriend Charlene. They've been married for (4) _____ years and they're still very happy. Charlene has replaced his Harley-Davidson motorcycle as the love of his life. He still has his bike – he's had it for (5) _____ years, but Charlene has made it clear who is number one now.

6   Complete these statements so that they are true for you.
1   I live in _____. I moved / was born there in _____ (date).
2   My favourite possession is my _____. I got it _____ years ago.
3   My best friend's name is _____. We met in _____ (date).
4   My favourite hobby is _____. I started it _____ years ago.

7   Write these questions.
1   Where / you / live? How long / you / live there?
    Where do you live? How long have you lived there?
2   What / your favourite possession? How long / you / have it?
3   What / your best friend's name? How long / you / know each other?
4   What / your favourite hobby? How long / you / do it?

8   Work with a partner. Ask and answer the questions in Ex 7. Use the information that you wrote in Ex 6 for your answers.

Weak forms

Pronunciation **1** Match these questions to the answers.

1 Where <u>do</u> you come from?   None. I prefer listening <u>to</u> music.
2 How long <u>have</u> you known your best friend?   Bangkok. It's the capital <u>of</u> Thailand.
3 How many instruments <u>can</u> you play?   <u>For</u> six years.

2 🔘 **03** Listen to how the <u>underlined</u> words are pronounced in the questions and answers in Ex 1. Are they stressed or not?

3 Work with a partner. Take turns to ask the questions in Ex 1. Give your own answers.

It's party time!

Listening **1** 🔘 **04** Look at the three photos. Where do you think each one is? What's happening in each one? Listen to three people talking about the festivals and check your ideas.

2 Listen again and complete the table with the words in the box.

Jerk chicken	~~Carnevale d'Ivrea~~	five days
1977	1808	Chiang Mai Flower Festival
February	throwing oranges	Notting Hill Carnival
fish and polenta	August	parade and beauty contest
three days	parade	February
calypso	two days	1964

	1	2	3
What's it called?	_Carnevale d'Ivrea_	_____	_____
When does it take place?	_____	_____	_____
How long does it last?	_____	_____	_____
When did it first take place?	_____	_____	_____
What is the main event?	_____	_____	_____
Is there any special food connected with it?	_____		_____
Is there any special music connected with it?			_____

Speaking **1** Think of a festival or celebration in your city or country. Look at the questions in Listening Ex 2 and think of an answer for each.

2 Work in groups and talk about your festival. Take a vote on the most interesting fact about each festival.

CD-ROM For more activities go to **Motion Unit 1**

2 Just do it

▲ free-running

LEARNING AIMS

- Can make comparative and superlative statements
- Can use phrases with *get*
- Can write a short story using sequencers

Hit the streets

Lead-in   **1**   Work in groups and discuss these questions.

1   Which of these sports have you tried / would you like to try?
2   What's the most unusual sport you've tried?

Listening   **1**   🔘 **05**   Listen to the interview and answer these questions.

1   Which of the sports in Lead-in Ex 1 are they discussing?
2   How many people does the interviewer talk to?

2   Complete the interviewer's questions with the words in the box. Listen again and answer the questions.

call   good   hurt   long   what   why

1   _____ is parkour?

2   Spider, how _____ have you been doing parkour?

3   Monkey, what do you _____ someone who does parkour?

4   Is parkour _____ for you?

5   Have you ever _____ yourself?

6   _____ do you do it?

3   What do you think of parkour? Would you like to try it?

▲ street basketball

▲ street football

Vocabulary and speaking   **1**   Put these words from Listening Ex 1 into the correct list.

| basketball   exercise   football   a game
scuba diving   skiing   a sport |
|---|

You **play:** _____

You **do:** _____

You **go:** _____

2   Add these sports to the lists in Ex 1.

| athletics   cycling   gymnastics   ice hockey   inline skating   judo   karate
skateboarding   squash   swimming   tennis |
|---|

3   Complete these statements with *play, do* or *go*.

1   Skydiving is the most dangerous sport you can _____.

2   Everybody should _____ at least one hour of exercise per day.

3   If you _____ swimming three times a week, you'll add ten years to your life.

4   There are some games that women shouldn't _____.

5   It's safer to _____ scuba diving than to _____ cycling.

4   Work with a partner and discuss the statements in Ex 4. Which do you agree with? Which do you disagree with? Give your reasons.

▲ inline skating

LANGUAGE STUDY

Comparatives and superlatives

1 Complete the table with words from Listening Ex 1. Look at listening script 5 on page 94 to help you.

Group	Adjective	Comparative	Superlative
1	young fast	_____ faster	the youngest _____
2	big fat	_____ fatter	the biggest _____
3	dangerous beautiful	_____ more / less beautiful	the most / least dangerous _____
4	good bad	_____ worse	the best _____
5	_____ easy	_____ easier	the scariest _____

2 Match these rules to each of the groups in the table in Ex 1.

  a   words ending in *-y* → *-ier* / *the -iest*

  b   irregular forms

  c   words ending in consonant–vowel–consonant
     → double the consonant + *-er* / *the -est*

  d   long words (two or more syllables)
     → *more* / *most* + adjective

  e   short words (one syllable) → *-er* / *the -est*

3 Look at these sentences. Complete the notes about form. Write *adjective*, *comparative* and *superlative*.

Form

1   Ben is **faster than** Michel.   _____ + *than*

2   Michel is **not as fast as** Ben.   *not as* + _____ + *as*

3   Ben is **the fastest**   *the* + _____
    person in the team.

▲ Ben   ▲ Michel

Grammar reference pages 90 and 91

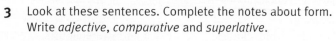

4 🔊 **06** Complete the text with the comparative form of the adjectives. Listen and check your answers. Look at the photo. Which one is Tanya?

I'm a bit (1 fat) _____ than my best friend, Tanya, but I'm still (2 good) _____ than her at tennis. I just find it (3 easy) _____ than she does, I suppose. Tanya's not as (4 tall) _____ as I am but she's very good-looking. She's (5 beautiful) _____ than any of the other women in our group, anyway.

5 🔊 **07** Listen to the biographies and complete these statements using the superlative form of the adjectives in the box.

bad   heavy   long   short   successful

1   Matt Coulter made the _____ jump on a quad bike.

2   Muggsy Bogues is the world's _____ ever basketball player.

3   Akebono is the _____ sportsman of all time.

4   Karine Ruby is the _____ World Cup snowboarding champion.

5   Eddie Edwards was the world's _____ ski jumper.

▲ Akebono

Get moving

Reading **1** 08 Read the story quickly and choose the best title. Explain your choice.

    a   Pollution problems in today's cities   b   The changing face of sports fashions

    c   Out of four wheels onto eight

I looked out of the window of my car. It was another hot day, and as usual I was sitting in a traffic jam, listening to the radio news. I was getting angry because the traffic wasn't moving. But then I looked in my mirror and saw a man on roller skates. He was dressed from head to toe in black, except for the small white earphones of his iPod. He was gorgeous. Then, as he came past, he looked at me and smiled. I hoped he hadn't seen me staring at him. As he moved away, I saw that he had *Why don't you try it?* on the back of his shirt. 'Yes,' I thought. 'Why don't I try it?' It would be the perfect way for me to get fit and maybe meet the mystery man in black.

The next day I went to a sports shop and bought a pair of skates. After that, I practised every weekend, and after a while I was ready to skate to work. I wasn't very good at first – I actually got lost on the first day and was fifteen minutes late for work. As time went on, I got better at skating and two years later, I'm still skating to work. It really is the best way to <u>get in shape</u>. I'm much slimmer these days. However, I never saw my mystery man again, but thanks to him, I gave up traffic jams and got into skating.

2 Read the text again and choose the correct alternative.

  1 The writer:
    a felt annoyed about the traffic jam.   b felt happy about the traffic jam.
    c didn't have strong feelings about the traffic jam.

  2 The skater was wearing:
    a black clothes.   b white clothes.   c black and white clothes.

  3 The writer thought the skater was:
    a silly.   b OK.   c good-looking.

  4 The skater:
    a ordered the writer to start skating.   b inspired the writer to start skating.
    c advised the writer to start skating.

  5 The writer:
    a wasn't very good at skating to begin with.
    b was immediately very good at skating.   c still can't skate very well.

  6 The writer has:
    a never been late for work since she started skating.
    b lost weight since she started skating.
    c made more friends since she started skating.

  7 The writer:
    a never wanted to see her mystery man again.
    b wanted to see her mystery man again, but didn't.
    c saw her mystery man again.

3 Work in groups and discuss these questions.

  1 What are the advantages and disadvantages of travelling to work on skates?
  2 Would you do it in your own town? Why? / Why not?
  3 Have you ever been inspired by someone to do something?

Phrases with *get*

Vocabulary **1** Look at the text on page 72 again and <u>underline</u> examples of phrases with *get / getting / got* (Example: *get in shape*). There are five more.

2 Match these definitions to the underlined phrases in Ex 1.

1 become slimmer = <u>*get in shape*</u>
2 became unsure of my location = _____
3 become healthy = _____
4 becoming annoyed = _____
5 improved = _____
6 started to enjoy = _____

3 Work with a partner and discuss these questions.

1 When was the last time you got angry? What about?
2 Have you ever got into something really quickly? What was it?
3 When was the last time you got lost? What happened?
4 What, in your opinion, is the best way to get fit and get in shape?
5 What have you got better at doing over the last twelve months?

4 Tell the class the most interesting piece of information you learned about your partner.

Writing **1** Look at these sentences from the text. Put the words in bold in the correct list.

__Then__, as he came past, he looked at me and smiled.
__The next day__ I went to a sports shop.
__After that__, I practised every weekend and __after a while__ I was ready to skate to work.
__However__, I never saw my mystery man again, but thanks to him, I gave up traffic jams.

Words that show time sequence	Words that show contrast
then	

2 Add these words to the lists in Ex 1.

although   finally   on the other hand   to begin with

3 You are going to write a story. Choose one of these topics.

1 A decision that changed my life
2 I looked out of the window … (continue the story)

4 Write your story in about 100 words. Use at least one word to show time sequence and at least one word to show contrast.

CD-ROM For more activities go to **Motion Unit 2**

3 On the road again

LEARNING AIMS

- Can make phrases using *say* and *tell*
- Can summarise a story
- Can discuss travel and holiday preferences

Save our soles

Lead-in **1** Work with a partner and discuss these questions.

1 Which of these reasons have you travelled for? When?
  - on business
  - on holiday
  - to visit family / friends

2 Can you think of any other reasons why people travel?

Reading **1** 🔊 **09** Read the three stories for one minute and match each one to a map.

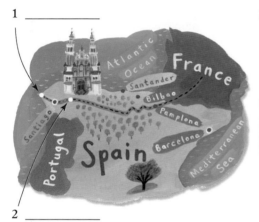

1 _____

2 _____

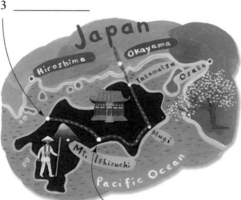

3 _____

4 _____

5 _____

6 _____

1 The Hajj, Mecca

Before we arrived in Mecca, we put on special white clothing that everyone wears for Hajj. My sister was very excited. She said, 'This experience will change us,' but I didn't feel the same. I was busy thinking about the crowds of people. I felt very worried. During the month of Hajj, there are more than four million pilgrims in the city.

When we arrived in Mecca, we circled the Kaaba (the most important building for Muslims) seven times. The next day, we left the city and walked five kilometres to Mina. The day after that, we walked the same distance to the Plain of Arafat. We returned on the fifth day and prepared to leave. My sister said that she felt different. I was surprised to discover that the journey had changed me, too. I honestly feel that I am a better person now.

2 The Camino de Santiago

Everybody told me to take comfortable walking boots, so I did. Most people do this pilgrimage for religious reasons, but we just wanted to see some beautiful countryside and get fit. We decided to fly to Santiago and then get the bus to Sarria. We planned to return from Sarria to Santiago on foot and continue until we reached Finisterre, the furthest point west.

Christian pilgrims usually stay at *refugios* (basic hostels), but we decided to stay at bed and breakfasts instead. The first day was fun, but on the second day my friend Susie started crying. 'I can't go on,' she told me. 'But we've only just started,' I said. Thankfully, things got better. We covered 25 km a day and completed our journey a week later. It wasn't a spiritual experience for me, but I lost weight and had a wonderful holiday.

3 The Shikoku Pilgrimage

I travelled by train to Takamatsu, in Shikoku, the smallest of the main islands. The Shikoku Pilgrimage consists of visiting 88 temples around the island. The pilgrims (*henro*) wear white clothes and a straw hat and carry a tall walking stick. One pilgrim told me that the journey around the island takes 60 days. But I only had three weeks, so I decided to follow part of the route. I started in Mugi and followed the coast around to Kochi. From there I walked over Mount Ishizuchi and ended my journey in Matsuyama. It was a life-changing experience for me. I met an old woman in one small village. 'You're the first foreign *henro* I've seen,' she said to me. There aren't many foreigners who make the pilgrimage, but I think everyone should try it once in their lives – it's good for the soul.

2 Work in groups of three. Each person in the group reads one story and completes the map with the missing place names.

3 Summarise your story to the other members of your group. Use the map to help you tell the story.

Example:
This is about a pilgrimage to Santiago in Spain. In this story, two people flew to Santiago and …

4 Work in your groups. Answer these questions with *1*, *2* or *3*. Sometimes more than one answer is possible.

   a In which story did someone feel nervous before they started?
   b In which story was / were the traveller(s) not interested in religion?
   c Where do the pilgrims wear white?
   d Which pilgrim spent the longest time on their journey?
   e Which pilgrim(s) travelled alone?
   f In which story did the experience change someone physically?
   g In which story did the experience change someone spiritually?

5 Work in your groups and discuss these questions.

   1 Which of the travellers do you think had the most interesting journey? Why?
   2 Would you consider doing this kind of journey? Why? / Why not?

Vocabulary

1 Complete these phrases from the text with the prepositions in the box.

at	by	in	on	to

| We travelled | (1) ____ | train. bus. plane. | We flew We got the train We went | (3) ____ | Santiago. Takamatsu. |
| | (2) ____ | foot. | | | |

| We arrived | (4) ____ | Mecca. Japan. |
| We stayed | (5) ____ | a lovely hotel. |

2 Complete these questions using the prepositions in Ex 1.

   1 Have you ever stayed _____ a five-star hotel?
   2 Would you like to fly _____ a tropical island, or would you prefer the mountains?
   3 What's the longest distance you've covered _____ foot in one day?
   4 What's the longest distance you've covered _____ train in one day?
   5 What's the longest period you've stayed _____ another country or city?

3 Work with a partner. Ask and answer the questions in Ex 2.

LANGUAGE STUDY

say and *tell*

1 Look at these sentences from the texts on page 74 and answer the questions. Write *a*, *b* or *c*.

a   **She said**, *'This experience will change us.'*   *'I can't go on,'* **she told me**.
   'You're the first foreign henro I've seen,' **she said to me**.

b   *My sister* **said that** *she felt different.*   *One pilgrim* **told me that** *the journey takes 60 days.*

c   *Everybody* **told me to take** *comfortable walking boots.*

1   Which pattern is used to give an order or piece of advice? ☐
2   Which pattern is used to report what someone said, using direct speech? ☐
3   Which pattern is used to report what someone said, using indirect speech? ☐

2 Look at the sentences in Ex 1 again. Complete these rules using *say* or *tell*.

1   When you use the verb _____, you usually include **who** you are speaking to. You can use a noun (John) or a pronoun (me, you, them, etc.).

2   When you use the verb _____, you **don't** usually include **who** you are speaking to. But when you do, you put *to* between the verb and the noun / pronoun.

Grammar reference page 91

3 Choose the correct alternative.

1   Carla _____, 'Let's go out tonight!'
   a   said   b   said her   c   tells   d   told

2   'That's a great idea,' Miki _____.
   a   say   b   said   c   told   d   said her

3   Carla _____ to meet her at 7.00.
   a   told   b   said Miki   c   says Miki   d   told Miki

4   She _____ they could take the bus.
   a   said Miki   b   tell Miki   c   told   d   said

5   Miki _____ that she preferred to walk.
   a   said Carla   b   say   c   told Carla   d   tells

6   Carla _____, 'It's quicker and safer by bus.'
   a   told   b   told her   c   said her   d   say

7   'Great. See you at 7.00, then,' Miki _____.
   a   said Carla   b   told to Carla   c   said to Carla   d   told

Take a break

Listening and vocabulary

1 Look at these five people. Guess which person likes which type of holiday.
   1   shopping
   2   doing sports and activities
   3   learning about the culture of the place
   4   doing nothing except relaxing
   5   home comforts and luxury

2 🔘 **10** Listen and check your ideas.

▲ Omar   ▲ Serena   ▲ Darren   ▲ Rebecca   ▲ Jun

3 Work with a partner. Complete the table for each person with the words in the boxes.

~~exotic~~		~~campsite~~		~~sightseeing~~
~~relaxing~~		B & B		white-water rafting
deluxe		two-star hotel		visiting museums
exciting		private villa		sunbathing
historical		resort		shopping
tropical paradise		self-catering apartment		

	Words to describe location		Types of accommodation		Holiday activities	
Omar	_____		*campsite*	_____	_____	
Serena	*relaxing*	_____	_____		_____	
Darren	*exotic*	_____	_____			
Rebecca			_____		_____	
Jun	_____		_____		*sightseeing*	_____

4 Listen again and check your answers.

5 Work with a partner and answer these questions about the five people.

   1   Who has travelled the most?   4   Which place does Jun like most?
   2   Who has travelled the least?   5   Who likes finding bargains?
   3   Who has the busiest lifestyle?

6 Which of these travellers do you think you are most similar to?

Speaking **1** You are going to find out what kind of traveller you are. Work with a partner. Student A turn to page 93. Student B turn to page 96.

2 Work with a partner. Ask and answer these questions. Note down your partner's answers.

   If you were given a free ticket to anywhere in the world …
   1   Where would you go? Who would you go with?
   2   How would you get there?
   3   What type of place would you stay in?
   4   What would you do during the day? during the evenings?
   5   How long would you spend on holiday?
   6   What would you take home as souvenirs?

3 Work with a new partner. Tell your new partner about your first partner's holiday. Your new partner should guess what kind of traveller your first partner is.

CD-ROM For more activities go to **Motion Unit 3**

4 Out and about

LEARNING AIMS

- Can talk about real and imaginary situations (conditionals)
- Can buy and return goods
- Can use shopping vocabulary

Trouble in store

Lead-in   **1**   Work in groups and discuss these questions.

1. Do you ever shop online?
2. What are the advantages and disadvantages?
3. Is it more or less enjoyable than shopping in shopping centres?

Listening and vocabulary

1   🔘 **11**   Listen to Paula's conversation in a shop and answer these questions.

1. What type of shop are they in?   2   What's the problem?

2   Which adjectives in the box would you use to describe: **a** Paula's manner? **b** the shop assistant's manner?

angry	confident	disappointed	helpful	polite	rude	shy	unhelpful

3   Look at these sentences from the conversation in Ex 1. Who said each one? Write *P* (Paula) or *S* (Shop assistant).

1. Can I help you? ☐
2. What seems to be the problem? ☐
3. I'd like a <u>refund</u>, please. ☐
4. Do you have a <u>receipt</u>? ☐
5. I think there's a <u>fault</u> in the machine. ☐
6. There is a one-year <u>warranty</u> on it. ☐
7. I'm sure the maker would agree to <u>replace</u> it. ☐
8. Can't I just <u>exchange</u> it here? ☐
9. I'm afraid that <u>model</u> is no longer <u>in stock</u>. ☐
10. I think I'll shop online next time. ☐

4   Listen again and check your answers.

5   Complete this summary of Paula's conversation with the underlined words in Ex 3.

Paula believed there was a (1) _____ with the item that she bought and asked the shop assistant for a (2) _____. The shop assistant checked her (3) _____ and told her that he couldn't help her. He then explained that, under the terms of the one-year (4) _____, the maker would probably (5) _____ it. Paula wanted to (6) _____ it, but the shop assistant told her that they didn't have the same (7) _____ (8) _____ anymore. Paula said that she would shop online next time.

6   Work in groups and discuss these questions.

1. Have you ever bought an item with a fault?
2. Have you ever exchanged anything for the same model, or replaced it with another? Did you need to show your receipt?
3. When was the last time you tried to buy something and found it was out of stock?
4. Which items do you own that are still under warranty?

Reading

1   Which search engines (e.g. Google) or websites (e.g. eBay, BBC) do you visit?

2   Match these words to their definitions.

1	look for information on a computer	a	auction
2	offer a particular amount of money for something	b	bid
3	a useful suggestion	c	browse
4	a public sale when things are sold to the people who offer the most money for them	d	tip

3   🔊 **12**   Read this article about eBay and match these headings to the paragraphs. (The completed text can be heard on track 12.)

Be patient – don't act too quickly	Close at the right time
Check reviews	Keep it simple
Do your research	Use plenty of images
~~Read the description of the item carefully~~	

The world's largest street market
Tim Mason takes us to the internet's largest auction site.

Welcome to eBay. It's so easy to use. You search for an item, place a bid and wait to see if you've won. Be careful, though – it's easy to get hooked. If I had more time, I'd spend it at eBay. It helps to know one or two things, too. Here are some essential tips for buyers and sellers.

Buyers

1   *Read the description of the item carefully*
    If you're not happy, you can return the item and get a full refund, but only if it is different from the way the seller described it.

2   _____
    You need to know a lot about an item before you buy it. A basic Google search can give you lots of information. Then you can search eBay more confidently.

3   _____
    If the seller has less than 98% positive feedback, be careful. Read all the comments about the seller carefully. Sometimes the negative comments are a result of a simple misunderstanding.

4   _____
    Watch and wait. If you bid too early, you'll push up the price. Bid late, but don't leave it too late.

Sellers

1   _____
    Most buyers browse the internet auction sites on Sunday evenings. So make sure your auction ends between 9 pm and 11 pm on a Sunday evening. If you do this, you'll get more money for your item.

2   _____
    You must provide enough photos of your item. People like to see what they're buying. Would you buy something if you couldn't see a picture of it? Show it from the front, the back, the side and from above.

3   _____
    Don't use flashing animation and large headings – it's not clever, it's annoying. You'll distract a buyer's attention if you use lots of colours. You want the buyer to look at your item, not at your animation.

4   According to the text, are these statements true or false?

1   You can get a refund if you change your mind and decide you don't want an item.
2   You can feel confident with a seller who has 98% (or more) positive feedback.
3   If you bid too early, the item will be more expensive in the end.
4   You can find cheaper items between 9 and 11 on Sunday evenings.
5   Your item will sell better if you use a variety of colours and font sizes.

5   Work with a partner and discuss these questions.

1   Would you ever bid for something in a public auction? Why? / Why not?
2   Have you ever won anything? What was it?
3   How often do you browse the internet?
4   Has anyone ever given you a good tip? What was it?

LANGUAGE STUDY

Talking about real and imaginary situations

First and second conditional

1   Look at these conditional sentences from the text on page 79 and answer the questions.

1st conditional

a   **If** you **bid** too early,   you**'ll push up** the price.

b   You**'ll distract** a buyer's attention   **if** you **use** lots of colours.

2nd conditional

c   **If** I **had** more time,   I**'d spend** it at eBay.

d   **Would** you **buy** something   **if** you **couldn't** see a picture of it?

Key ▭ = If clause   ▭ = conditional clause

1   Which sentences are talking about an imaginary situation?
2   Which sentences are talking about a real / possible future situation?

2   Look at the sentences in Ex 1 again. Tick (✓) a box in the table, depending on whether the rule relates to the 1st conditional, the 2nd conditional or both of them.

		1st	2nd	both
1	There are two parts: the *If* clause and the conditional clause.	☐	☐	☐
2	In the *If* clause, the verb is usually in the present tense.	☐	☐	☐
3	The conditional clause usually contains *will / 'll / won't* + infinitive.	☐	☐	☐
4	In the *If* clause, the verb is usually in the past tense.	☐	☐	☐
5	The conditional clause usually contains *would / 'd / wouldn't* + infinitive.	☐	☐	☐
6	The *If* clause can come first or second in the sentence.	☐	☐	☐
7	If the *If* clause comes first, the two parts are separated by a comma.	☐	☐	☐

Grammar reference page 91

3   Look at these shopping slogans. They are all first conditional sentences. Choose the correct alternatives.

1   We *refund* / *'ll refund* the difference if you *find* / *'ll* find one cheaper.
2   If you *eat* / *'ll eat* an apple a day, you *'re* / *'ll be* healthy.
3   You *pay* / *'ll pay* lower insurance if you *buy* / *'ll buy* one of our cars.
4   You *'re* / *'ll be* safe all the time if you *wear* / *'ll wear* an Escher helmet.
5   If you *don't* / *won't* brush your teeth with Smile, they *don't* / *won't* stay white.

4   Complete this story, according to the rules for second conditional sentences. Choose the correct alternative.

It's fun to dream about what I (1) *did* / *'d do* if I (2) *had* / *'d have* lots of money. I (3) *bought* / *'d buy* a Ferrari if I (4) *could choose* / *would choose* the car of my dreams. If I (5) *had* / *'d have* a Ferrari, I (6) *drove* / *'d drive* it straight to the shops. I (7) *spent* / *'d spend* hours buying designer clothes, if I (8) *was* / *'d be* in the right mood. Then, if I (9) *had* / *would have* time, I (10) *went* / *'d go* for a coffee with my A-list celebrity friends. At the end of the day, if I (11) *felt like* / *'d feel* like staying in, I (12) *had* / *'d have* a long, relaxing bath before going to bed.

5   🔊 13 Listen and check your answers.

6 Which of these questions do you think are asking about imaginary situations? Which are asking about real and possible situations? Complete the first half of each question with the verb in the correct form and *'ll / will* or *'d / would* in the second half.

1 If the weather (be) _____ good next weekend, do you think you _____ go shopping?

2 If you (go) _____ shopping next weekend, what _____ you buy?

3 If you (have) _____ unlimited money, what _____ you spend it on?

4 If you (find) _____ some money lying on the street, what _____ you do?

5 If you (buy) _____ a fake designer bag, _____ you tell everybody it was real?

6 If you (go) _____ out tonight, how _____ you get there?

7 Work with a partner. Ask and answer the questions in Ex 6.

What do I say?

Reading **1** Work with a partner. Choose the correct answer for each question in the shopping quiz.

opping

QUIZ

1 **What do you say in a shop when you want to walk around but not buy anything?**
   a I'm just watching, thanks.
   b I'm just seeing, thanks.
   c I'm just looking, thanks.

2 **Complete the student's question: 'Do you do students' ...**
   a discounts?'
   b reductions?'
   c price cuts?'

3 **You want to know if you can return an item to the shop if you're not happy. What do you ask the shop assistant?**
   a Can I take it back if it's not right?
   b Can I bring it back if it's not right?
   c Can I go back if it's not right?

4 **You want to use your credit card. What do you ask?**
   a Do you take credit cards?
   b Did you take my credit cards?
   c Who took my credit cards?

5 **You have an item that you want to return. What does the shop assistant ask you?**
   a Do you have the recipe?
   b Do you have the ticket?
   c Do you have the receipt?

6 **You want to know if an item is included in a special low-price offer. What do you ask?**
   a Is this in the sale?   b Is this cheap?
   c Is this sold?

7 **You see an item which is cheaper than its usual price. What <u>wouldn't</u> you say?**
   a This is a bargain.   b This is pricey.
   c This is a good buy.

Writing and speaking **1** Work with a partner. You are going to write a short dialogue between a customer and a shop assistant. Follow these instructions.

Step 1: Choose an adjective from the box to describe each of your characters. As you prepare your dialogue, your characters should act like their adjective (so if you choose *helpful* for the shop assistant, then your shop assistant should be helpful).

angry   bored   confident   disappointed   helpful   suspicious   unhelpful

Step 2: Think about these questions:
1 What kind of shop are they in?
2 Is the customer buying something or returning it?
3 Is there a problem?
4 About how old is the customer? And the shop assistant?
Use phrases from the quiz and as much vocabulary from other parts of this unit as you can.

Step 3: When you have finished preparing your dialogue, read it to another pair. They guess the adjective you chose for each of your characters.

CD-ROM For more activities go to **Motion Unit 4**

5 Review

Lead-in **1** Work with a partner and discuss these questions.

  1   How do you travel to work / college? Do you enjoy the journey? Why? / Why not?
  2   Would you like a driving job? Why? / Why not?

Language study

1 Correct the mistakes in the magazine article.

In this week's article about jobs and people we look at people who work with different forms of transport.

Aleksy, 43, is a lorry driver from Warsaw in Poland. He (1) *said me* ____*said*____, 'I've been a lorry driver (2) *since* _____ about twenty years and I really enjoy it. Some people don't like driving, but I find it very relaxing. That's probably because I listen to music while I'm travelling. I often travel abroad, for example, next week I'm going to Edinburgh in Scotland. If I arrive there early in the evening, I (3) *'d* _____ find a hotel or a B & B. If I (4) *got* _____ there late, I'll just sleep in my lorry. It's like my second home!'

Joaquim, 35, is a bus driver from Guatemala City in Guatemala. He (5) *told* _____, 'I've been driving buses (6) *for* _____ I was thirty. I used to work in an office and before that I worked in a shop, but being a bus driver is the (7) *better* _____ job I've had. I like meeting people and travelling about. Of course I sit down a lot in my job, so I do a lot of exercise in my spare time. I like playing football and I go swimming a lot. If I changed my job, I (8) *'ll* _____ probably be a train driver. My problem is – I don't like staying in one place!'

Hazel Green, 25, is a taxi driver from London. She (9) *said* _____ me, 'I (10) *was* _____ a taxi driver for about two years. My dad was a taxi driver too and this is his cab. Most of the other drivers are older (11) *as* _____ me, but they're all really nice. When I (12) *'ve begun* _____, I was really nervous because London seemed so big. These days, I'm a lot more confident. I love meeting people and most passengers are really (13) *friendlier* _____. Being a taxi driver is a great job. If I (14) *win* _____ the lottery, I'd probably still drive my taxi!'

2 Use the information and the prompts to write a text about Sarah Harris.

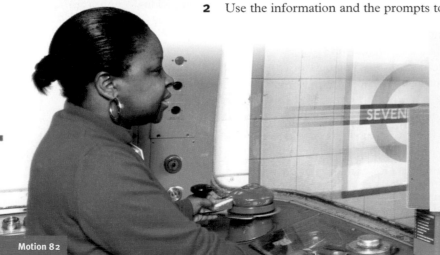

> **Name:** Sarah Harris
> **Age:** 32
> **Town:** Liverpool (moved there in 1999)
> **Job:** underground train driver – five years (interesting)
> **Previous jobs:** shop assistant (tiring), secretary (boring)
> **Ambition:** flying lessons

Vocabulary

1 Work in groups. Read how to play 'Journey', then play the game.

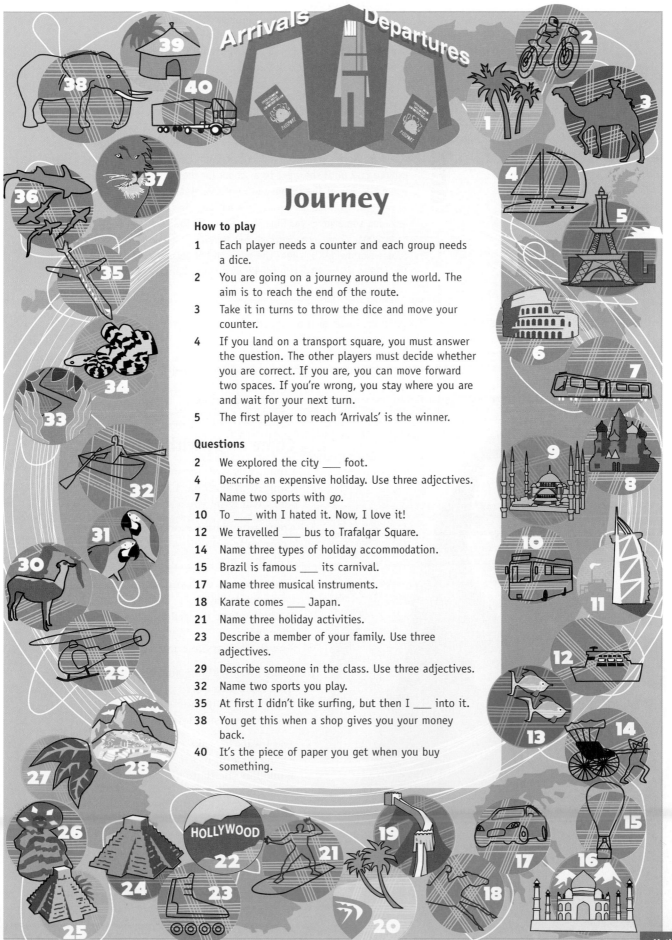

Journey

How to play

1 Each player needs a counter and each group needs a dice.

2 You are going on a journey around the world. The aim is to reach the end of the route.

3 Take it in turns to throw the dice and move your counter.

4 If you land on a transport square, you must answer the question. The other players must decide whether you are correct. If you are, you can move forward two spaces. If you're wrong, you stay where you are and wait for your next turn.

5 The first player to reach 'Arrivals' is the winner.

Questions

2 We explored the city ___ foot.

4 Describe an expensive holiday. Use three adjectives.

7 Name two sports with *go*.

10 To ___ with I hated it. Now, I love it!

12 We travelled ___ bus to Trafalgar Square.

14 Name three types of holiday accommodation.

15 Brazil is famous ___ its carnival.

17 Name three musical instruments.

18 Karate comes ___ Japan.

21 Name three holiday activities.

23 Describe a member of your family. Use three adjectives.

29 Describe someone in the class. Use three adjectives.

32 Name two sports you play.

35 At first I didn't like surfing, but then I ___ into it.

38 You get this when a shop gives you your money back.

40 It's the piece of paper you get when you buy something.

Song

1 Read the factfile and answer these questions.

    1   What instruments does Norah Jones play?

    2   As a young person, which singer influenced Norah Jones?

    3   When did she become really interested in jazz?

    4   Who did she and her group sign a contract with in 2001?

    5   What was the name of her second album?

> **factfile**
>
> Singer, pianist and guitarist Norah Jones performs an interesting mix of jazz and traditional pop music. Norah was born on March 30, 1979, in New York City and is the daughter of musician, Ravi Shankar. When she was a young teenager, Norah enjoyed the music of Billie Holiday, but she didn't really explore jazz until she went to a school for the Performing and Visual Arts. While she was at the school she won several music awards. She then began to write her own songs and formed a group. In October 2000, the group recorded some songs for Blue Note Records. The jazz label signed them in early 2001. *Come away with me* was Norah's first album and it sold 18 million copies worldwide. In 2004, she released her second album, *Feels like home*. The album mixes 70s style tracks with blues, country and jazz.

2 Work with a partner. Look at these words and predict what you think the song is about. Share your ideas with the class.

come away   night   bus   walk in fields   kiss   mountain top   wake up   safe

3 🔘 **14** Listen to the song and check your predictions.

Come away with me

Come away with me in the night
Come away with me
And I will write you a song

Come away with me on a bus
Come away with me where they can't tempt us
With their lies

I want to walk with you
On a cloudy day
In fields where the yellow grass grows
knee high
So won't you try to come

Come away with me and we'll kiss
On a mountain top
Come away with me
And I'll never stop loving you

And I want to wake up with the rain
Falling on a tin roof
While I'm safe there in your arms
So all I ask is for you
To come away with me in the night
Come away with me

4 Answer these questions.

1 When does the singer want to go away?
2 What does she promise to write if the person comes with her?
3 How does she suggest they should travel?
4 What kind of weather does she mention?
5 What kind of places does she want to go to?

5 Do you think it is a romantic song? Why? / Why not?

Speaking: a survey

1 Work with a partner. You are going to prepare a shopping survey. Follow the instructions.

Step 1: **Prepare the information you need**

🔘 **15** Listen to the example shopping survey. Which information is mentioned?

name	occupation	age	credit card	favourite shop	amount spent
how often the person complains		places the person would like to go shopping			

Look at the questionnaire. Write questions for each piece of information that is needed.

Examples:
Amount of money spent on clothes every month: *How much do you spend on clothes every month?*
Usual method of payment: *How do you usually pay?*

		Person 1	Person 2
1	Name	_____	_____
2	Occupation	_____	_____
3	Age	_____	_____
4	Number of times you go shopping, not including for food (e.g. every weekend, twice a month)	_____	_____
5	Amount of money you spend on clothes / entertainment / electronic goods every month	_____	_____
6	Usual method of payment (e.g. cash, cheques, credit card)	_____	_____
7	Number of times you've done internet shopping	_____	_____
8	Places you'd like to go shopping in (e.g. London, Paris, New York)	_____	_____
9	How often you complain and why (e.g. Often, if the service is bad. Never, I hate complaining.)	_____	_____
10	_____	_____	_____
11	_____	_____	_____
12	_____	_____	_____

Step 2: **Prepare extra questions for a survey**
Add three more questions to the questionnaire.

Step 3: **Perform your survey**
• Ask two students your questions.
• Answer other students' questions. You can give true or imaginary answers.

Step 4: **Discuss your survey results**
When all of the groups have finished, vote to decide which person interviewed wins in the following categories: the biggest shopaholic, the biggest internet spender, the most frequent complainer.

Extra practice

Unit 1

1 Complete these sentences with the prepositions in the box.

> for   from   in   of   with

1 Bhangra is traditional Asian music mixed _____ modern dance music.

2 Reggae arrived _____ Europe in the 1960s.

3 When people hear Samba music, they usually think _____ the Rio carnival.

4 Louis Armstrong came _____ New Orleans.

5 The Notting Hill Carnival is famous _____ calypso music.

2 Match the musical instruments to the pictures.

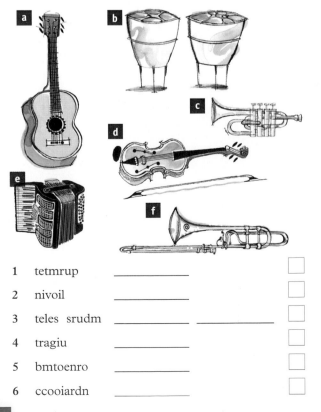

| a | b | c |
| d | | |

1 tambourine ☐   3 piano ☐

2 flute ☐   4 saxophone ☐

3 Rearrange these letters to find six musical instruments. Match them to the pictures

a	b
e	c
	d
	f

1 tetmrup _____ ☐

2 nivoil _____ ☐

3 teles srudm _____ _____ ☐

4 tragiu _____ ☐

5 bmtoenro _____ ☐

6 ccooiardn _____ ☐

4 Complete the text with the present perfect simple form of the verbs.

> Bhangra is a lively form of traditional music with dance that comes from India and Pakistan. There, people (1 perform) _____ Bhangra for thousands of years. They traditionally performed it when celebrating the harvest, but then it became a part of other celebrations such as weddings. Bhangra (2 be) _____ popular in other countries for a long time too. In fact, people worldwide (3 enjoy) _____ Bhangra since the 70s. However, musicians (4 change) _____ Bhangra since it became popular. They've mixed it with hip-hop, house and reggae. Bhangra Knights are a popular group. They (5 be) _____ famous since their song *Husan* was used for a Peugeot 206 car advert in 2003.

5 Complete these sentences in two different ways using *for* and *since*.

Example:
I've known my best friend …
for *five years* .
since *I was eighteen* .

1 I've known my best friend …
for _____.
since _____.

2 I haven't been on holiday …
for _____.
since _____.

3 I've lived in this town …
for _____.
since _____.

4 I've had the shoes I'm wearing …
for _____.
since _____.

5 I haven't eaten anything …
for _____.
since _____.

Unit 2

1 Tick (✓) the correct sentences. Rewrite the incorrect sentences using *play*, *do* or *go*.

Example:
I sometimes play squash with my best friend. ✓
I ~~do~~ football every weekend. *I play football every weekend.*

1 My sister goes a lot of exercise every day.
2 I often go inline skating with my friends.
3 My uncle does golf at weekends.
4 I go karate every Saturday morning.
5 I'd love to go ice hockey.
6 A lot of people go running in our local park.
7 We didn't play athletics at our school.
8 You can go scuba diving in our local swimming pool.

2 Complete the text about the brothers. Use the comparative or superlative form of the adjectives.

Raul   Pepe

Raul and Pepe are twins. Raul was born first. He's thirty minutes (1 old) _____ than his brother. He was a very small baby and when they were children, Pepe was (2 big) _____ than Raul. But now, Raul is taller than Pepe and he has (3 long) _____ legs. This means he is (4 fast) _____ than Pepe. In fact, Raul is a really good runner. He's (5 good) _____ runner in his athletics club. Raul also likes doing extreme sports. He likes free-running and skateboarding, but ski jumping is probably (6 dangerous) _____ sport he does. Raul is good at these sports because he isn't as (7 heavy) _____ as Pepe. Pepe is a bit fat! But, in fact, Pepe is (8 successful) _____ than Raul because he's a professional footballer. One day, he'll play for Spain.

3 Write a comparative and a superlative sentence for each group of words using the adjective.

Example:
Extreme sports: skateboarding / parkour / ski jumping (dangerous)
Parkour is more dangerous than skateboarding.
Ski jumping is the most dangerous extreme sport.

1 Sports: basketball / tennis / golf (interesting)
_____
_____
_____

2 Actors: Brad Pitt / Leonardo DiCaprio / Tom Cruise (handsome)
_____
_____
_____

3 Actresses: Nicole Kidman / Angelina Jolie / Halle Berry (pretty)
_____
_____
_____

4 Complete the text with the words in the box.

> after that   although   but   finally   however
> the next day

Last Friday night, I was feeling bored and a bit lonely. I decided to join a gym to (a) <u>become healthy</u> and meet more people. (1) _____ I went to the local sports club. As I wanted to (b) <u>become slimmer,</u> I decided to run there. I took a map because I didn't want to (c) <u>become unsure of my location</u>. I also took a bottle of water and my iPod. I left the house and bumped into an old friend called Sarah. We decided to go for a coffee and have a chat. (2) _____ I hadn't seen her for ages, we got on really well and talked for a long time. (3) _____, we had lunch. (4) _____ I went to the gym in the late afternoon, (5) _____ when I got there, it was closed. (6) _____, I didn't (d) <u>become annoyed</u>. I decided to go for a run round the park. I have to admit I really (e) <u>started to enjoy</u> it and now I'm a big running fan.

5 Replace the <u>underlined</u> words in the text in Ex 4 with five of the expressions in the box.

> get angry   got better   get fit   get in shape
> get into   get lost

Unit 3

1 Complete the text with the prepositions in the box.

> at by in on to

We had a fantastic holiday (1) _____ America last year. From Los Angeles, we flew (2) _____ Las Vegas and then we travelled (3) _____ taxi from the airport to The Strip (the main street). We stayed (4) _____ a fantastic hotel and spent two days visiting the sights and the casinos! We went (5) _____ car (rented) for some of the time, but most of the time we explored the place (6) _____ foot. On our third day, we went on a trip to the Grand Canyon. We travelled there (7) _____ helicopter and arrived (8) _____ the canyon in a really short time. We had a picnic and explored for a couple of hours. What a great experience! We got the bus back (9) _____ Las Vegas and on the journey saw some fantastic scenery.

2 Choose the correct alternative.

1 Sarah *said / told*, 'I'd like to go to Italy this year.'

2 Tim *told / told to* her he didn't like flying.

3 Sarah *said / said to* him, 'We can go by train.'

4 Tim *told / said* her that he didn't like long journeys.

5 Sarah *said / told to*, 'We can stay in a hotel in Paris for a few days and then travel again.'

6 Tim *said / told* her he didn't like hotels.

7 'I've got friends in France. We can go there,' Sarah *said / told* to him.

8 Tim *said / told* to her that he didn't speak French.

9 Sarah *said / said to* Tim, 'All right. My parents live in London. Let's go there.'

10 Tim *told her / told her to* book the holiday.

3 Read the descriptions of the people and the adverts for holiday places. Replace the underlined phrases with the words in the box.

> campsites   deluxe   paradise   sunbathing
> self-catering apartments   sightseeing

1 Bill and Brenda are in their fifties. They want a short break. They like <u>looking at famous buildings</u>.

2 Sandip and Ayesha have just got married. They're in their twenties and want to do some exciting sports.

3 Carla and Wen like <u>lying in the sun</u> by the sea. They'd like to stay in a <u>really expensive</u> hotel.

4 Jen and Peter have one child. They're looking for a holiday in the sun with lots to do.

5 Ben and Erica have three children. They want a cheap holiday with plenty of exciting activities.

a   **Places for tents in Wales**
- Trips to the beach – walking and hiking
- Friendly atmosphere and evening events at inexpensive prices

b   **Adventures in the Rocky Mountains**
- Camping, hiking, white-water rafting

c   **Portugal, Spain, France, Greece**
- <u>Accommodation with cooking facilities</u> in beautiful sea towns around the Mediterranean
- Private pools. Excellent restaurants.
- Evening entertainment. Children's day camps available

d   **City breaks**
- Two-day break in Paris
- Three-star hotel close to the Eiffel Tower and other attractions

e   **Stay in <u>a beautiful place</u>**
- Relax in Barbados – five-star hotel by the beach
- Superb food and entertainment

4 Look at the descriptions and the adverts again. Match the people to the types of holidays.

1 ☐   2 ☐   3 ☐   4 ☐   5 ☐

Unit 4

1 Match these words to their definitions.

> exchange   fault   in stock   model   receipt
> refund   warranty

1   when you get your money back = _____

2   the piece of paper to show you have paid for
something = _____

3   a problem with the item that stops it from working
properly = _____

4   a company's promise to repair or replace an item
if it does not work = _____

5   change something for something else
= _____

6   a particular type or kind of something
= _____

7   items that are available to buy in a shop
= _____

2 Complete the dialogue using the words in Ex 1.

Shop assistant: Can I help you?

Karen: Yes, please. I bought this radio last
week, but it has a (1) _____.
There's no sound.

Shop assistant: Do you have the (2) _____?

Karen: No, I don't. I've lost it, but I paid by
credit card. Here's my statement.

Shop assistant: All right, that's fine. Now, it had one
year's (3) _____ so we can
send it back to the maker.

Karen: No, thank you. That will take too
long.

Shop assistant: Would you like to (4) _____
it for another radio? I think we have
another one (5) _____.

Karen: No. I don't think this can be a very
good (6) _____. I'd like my
money back.

Shop assistant: I'm sorry, madam, we can't give a
(7) _____ without a receipt.

3 Correct the most likely mistake in these conditional
sentences.

Example:
        won
If you ~~win~~ a million dollars, would you give up work?

1   If you eat healthy food, you'd live longer.

2   If you went out this week, who will you go with?

3   If you met the Queen of England, what will you
say?

4   Will you phone me tonight if you had time?

5   If you see someone stealing from a shop, what
would you do?

4 Write a sentence about each situation. Use the first or
second conditional.

Example:
If you won the lottery, what would you do?
If I won the lottery, I'd go on a long holiday.

1   If it's sunny on Saturday, what will you do?

_____

_____

2   If you lost your wallet, would would you do?

_____

_____

3   If you go out this weekend, where will you go?

_____

_____

4   If you met an A-list celebrity, what would you say?

_____

_____

5 Complete the puzzle with words from Unit 4. What's
the extra word? _____

							B			
1										
2									G	
3					U					
4	S			I						
5									D	
6		N					T			
7	R									
8						P				

Clues

1   It's an offer to pay a particular amount of money
for something.

2   It's how you'd feel if someone hit your car and
ran away.

3   It's a public sale where things are sold to the
people who offer the most money for them.

4   It's how you feel when you lose.

5   It's the opposite of polite.

6   You are this when you believe in your own
ability.

7   It's the verb to look for information on a
computer.

8   It's a useful suggestion or piece of information
that someone gives you.

Grammar reference

Unit 1

for and *since* with the present perfect

You use the present perfect with *for* and *since* to talk about actions which started in the past and continue until now.

for

You use *for* with the present perfect to refer to how long something has been happening up to now.

We've lived here for ten years. (We started living here ten years ago and we're still here.)

since

You use *since* with the present perfect to refer to a point at the beginning of a period of time, which usually leads up to now.

I've been here since Friday. (I arrived on Friday and I am still here.)

for	since
a week	I was born
a few minutes	last week
ages	I was young
three days	2005
a long time	last Easter
25 years	24th December
two months	three o'clock

Unit 2

Comparatives and superlatives

There are five main types of comparative and superlative adjectives:

Present perfect simple

> have / has ('ve /'s) + past participle

*They've **known** each other since they were children.*

You usually use the present perfect simple with *for* and *since* to emphasise that you are talking about a completed action or a permanent state.

You've changed since last summer. (completed action – the result is evident now)

I've lived here for six years. (I started living here six years ago and I still live here. The use of the simple form makes it sound like a permanent state.)

Present perfect continuous

> have / has ('ve /'s) + been + -ing form of the verb

*I've **been waiting** here for ages.*

You usually use the present perfect continuous with *for* and *since* to emphasise that you are talking about an activity, repeated action or a temporary state.

*I've **been waiting** since four o'clock this afternoon.* (an activity leading up to now)

*She's **been coming** to English classes for two years.* (a repeated action leading up to now)

*I've **been living** here for two years.* (I started living here two years ago and I still live here. Here the use of the continuous form makes it sound like a temporary state.)

The continuous form is not usually used with verbs which refer to state or feeling.
~~I've been knowing him since last year.~~
I've known him since last year.
~~She's been liking him for years.~~
She's liked him for years.

	Group	Adjective	Comparative	Superlative
1	Short words (usually one syllable)	young fast	young**er** fast**er**	**the** young**est** **the** fast**est**
2	Words ending in consonant–vowel–consonant	big fat	big**ger** fat**ter**	the big**gest** the fat**test**
3	Long words (two or more syllables)	dangerous beautiful	**more / less** dangerous **more / less** beautiful	**the most / least** dangerous **the most / least** beautiful
4	Irregular forms	good bad	**better** **worse**	**the best** **the worst**
5	Words ending in -y	scary easy	scar**ier** eas**ier**	the scar**iest** the eas**iest**

Compare:
younger, older (comparative)
youngest, oldest (superlative)
and:
more beautiful, less beautiful (comparative)
most beautiful, least beautiful (superlative)

For adjectives from Group 3 (long words), you don't need a different adjective, you only need to change *more / most* to *less / least*.

not as ... as / comparative + than

When comparing two things, you use the comparative adjective followed by *than*. You use *not as* + (adjective) + *as* in negative comparisons.
*Ben is faster **than** Michel. = Michel is **not as fast as** Ben.*

Unit 3

say and tell

Both *say* and *tell* have meanings that are about speaking to other people, but you use them in different ways.

tell

When you use verb *tell*, you usually include <u>who</u> you are speaking to. You can use a noun (*John*) or pronoun (*you, him, her, them, someone*, etc.).

These are some common patterns using *tell*:
Tell <u>someone</u> to do something (give advice or orders)
*Mum **told** <u>me</u> to do my homework.*

Tell <u>someone</u> something (pass on information)
*She **told** <u>Tim</u> the whole story.*

Tell <u>someone</u> something (reporting)
*They **told** <u>her</u> (that) they didn't need her anymore.*

say

When you use verb *say*, you don't usually include who you are speaking to. But when you do, you put <u>to</u> between the verb and the noun / pronoun.

These are some common patterns, using *say*:
Say something
*He **said**, 'Pleased to meet you.'*

Say something <u>to</u> someone
*Paula **said** <u>to</u> him, 'I'm sure we've met before.'*

Say something (reporting)
*He **said** (that) he was going to come to the party.*

Reporting

When you use *say* and *tell* to report what someone else said, you can use *that* if you want. Also the verb which follows *say* or *tell* is often 'backshifted' (e.g. present ǂ past, past ǂ past perfect (see *Move Intermediate*), etc.) to emphasise that it is reported speech.
Direct speech *Sue: 'I **feel** great.'*
Reported speech *Sue said (that) she **felt** great.*

If you want to report something that is still true, there is no need to 'backshift'.
Direct speech *Pilgrim: 'The journey **takes** 60 days.'*
Reported speech *The pilgrim told me (that) the journey **takes** 60 days.*

Unit 4

Talking about real and imaginary situations

First conditional

You use the first conditional to talk about real or possible situations in the future.

> *If* + (present tense), *will ('ll) / won't*
> ***If** you **come** too early, you**'ll** have to help.*

There are two parts to a first conditional sentence: the 'if' clause (*If you come too early,*) and the conditional clause (*you'll have to help*). In the 'if' clause, the verb is usually in the present tense. The conditional clause contains *will / 'll* or *won't*.

If the 'if' clause comes second in the sentence, there is no comma.
You'll have to help if you come too early.

Second conditional

You use the second conditional to talk about imaginary situations.

> *If* + (past tense), *would ('d) / wouldn't*
> ***If I had** more time, **I'd** help.*

There are two parts to a second conditional sentence: the 'if' clause (*If I had more time,*) and the conditional clause (*I'd help*). In the 'if' clause, the verb is usually in the past tense. The conditional clause usually contains *would / 'd* or *wouldn't*.

If the 'if' clause comes second in the sentence, there is no comma.
I'd help if I had more time.

Wordlist

*** the 2,500 most common English words, ** very common words, * fairly common words

Unit 1

accordion *n* /əˈkɔːdiən/
arrive in *v* /əˈraɪv ɪn/ ***
beauty contest *n* /ˈbjuːti ˌkɒntest/
calypso *n* /kəˈlɪpsəʊ/
carnival *n* /ˈkɑːnɪvl/
combine *v* /kəmˈbaɪn/ ***
come from *v* /ˈkʌm ˌfrɒm, frəm/ ***
culture *n* /ˈkʌltʃə/ ***
(the) elderly *n* /(ði) ˈeldəli/ ***
event *n* /ɪˈvent/ ***
famous for *adj* /ˈfeɪməs ˌfɔː, fə/ ***
fasting *n* /ˈfɑːstɪŋ/
festival *n* /ˈfestɪvl/ ***
flute *n* /fluːt/
folk *adj* /fəʊk/
guitar *n* /ɡɪˈtɑː/ ***
instrument *n* /ˈɪnstrʊmənt/ ***
jazz *n* /dʒæz/ *
(the) middle-aged *n* /(ðə) ˌmɪdl ˈeɪdʒd/ *
mix with *v* /ˈmɪks wɪð/ ***
mixture *n* /ˈmɪkstʃə/ ***
musical *adj* /ˈmjuːzɪkl/ **
parade *n* /pəˈreɪd/ *
piano *n* /piˈænəʊ/ **
possession *n* /pəˈzeʃn/ **
rhythm *n* /ˈrɪðm/ ***
roots *n pl* /ruːts/ ***
samba *n* /ˈsæmbə/
saxophone *n* /ˈsæksəfəʊn/
slave *n* /sleɪv/ **
sound *n* /saʊnd/ ***
steel drums *n* /ˌstiːl ˈdrʌmz/
take place *phrase* /ˌteɪk ˈpleɪs/
tambourine *n* /ˌtæmbəˈriːn/
think of *v* /ˈθɪŋk ˌɒv, əv/ ***
throw *v* /θrəʊ/ ***
traditional *adj* /trəˈdɪʃn(ə)l/ ***
trombone *n* /trɒmˈbəʊn/
trumpet *n* /ˈtrʌmpɪt/ *
violin *n* /ˌvaɪəˈlɪn/ *

Unit 2

a game *n* /ə ˈɡeɪm/ ***
achieve *v* /əˈtʃiːv/ ***
advantage *n* /ədˈvɑːntɪdʒ/ ***
advise *v* /ədˈvaɪz/ ***
after that *phrase* /ˌɑːftə ˈðæt/
although *conj* /ɔːlˈðəʊ/ ***
annoyed *adj* /əˈnɔɪd/ **
athletics *n* /æθˈletɪks/ *
basketball *n* /ˈbɑːskɪtbɔːl/ *
but *conj* /bʌt, bət/ ***
champion *n* /ˈtʃæmpiən/ ***
cycling *n* /ˈsaɪklɪŋ/ **
dangerous *adj* /ˈdeɪndʒərəs/ ***
despite *prep* /dɪˈspaɪt/ ***
disadvantage *n* /ˌdɪsədˈvɑːntɪdʒ/ **
exercise *n* /ˈeksəsaɪz/ ***
feel *v* /fiːl/ ***
finally *adv* /ˈfaɪnəli/ ***
football *n* /ˈfʊtbɔːl/ ***
get angry *v* /ˌɡet ˈæŋɡri/
get better at *v* /ˌɡet ˈbetər ət, ˈbetə ət/
get fit *v* /ˌɡet ˈfɪt/
get in shape *v* /ˌɡet ɪn ˈʃeɪp/
get into *v* /ˌɡet ˈɪntuː, ˈɪntə/
get lost *v* /ˌɡet ˈlɒst/ **
gymnastics *n* /dʒɪmˈnæstɪks/
health *n* /helθ/ ***
heavy *adj* /ˈhevi/ ***
height *n* /haɪt/ ***
however *conj* /haʊˈevə/ ***
hurt *v* /hɜːt/ ***
ice hockey *n* /ˈaɪs ˌhɒki/
immediately *adv* /ɪˈmiːdiətli/ ***
inline skating *n* /ˌɪnlaɪn ˈskeɪtɪŋ/

inspire *v* /ɪnˈspaɪə/ **
judo *n* /ˈdʒuːdəʊ/
karate *n* /kəˈrɑːti/
lose weight *v* /ˌluːz ˈweɪt/
on the other hand *phrase* /ˌɒn ði ˌʌðə ˈhænd/
onto *prep* /ˈɒntuː, ˈɒntə/ ***
parkour *n* /pɑːˈkɔː/
quad bike *n* /ˈkwɒd ˌbaɪk/
racket *n* /ˈrækɪt/ *
rugby *n* /ˈrʌɡbi/ *
scuba diving *n* /ˈskuːbə ˌdaɪvɪŋ/
skateboarding *n* /ˈskeɪtˌbɔːdɪŋ/
skater *n* /ˈskeɪtə/
ski jumper *n* /ˈskiː ˌdʒʌmpə/
skiing *n* /ˈskiːɪŋ/
skydiving *n* /ˈskaɪˌdaɪvɪŋ/
snowboarding *n* /ˈsnəʊˌbɔːdɪŋ/
sport *n* /spɔːt/ ***
squash *n* /skwɒʃ/
successful *adj* /səkˈsesfl/ ***
sumo wrestling *n* /ˈsuːməʊ ˌreslɪŋ/
swimming *n* /ˈswɪmɪŋ/ *
tennis *n* /ˈtenɪs/ **
the next day *phrase* /ðə ˌnekst ˈdeɪ/
then *conj* /ðen/ ***
to begin with *phrase* /tə bɪˈɡɪn ˌwɪð/
traffic jam *n* /ˈtræfɪk ˌdʒæm/
urban *adj* /ˈɜːbən/ ***
wheel *n* /wiːl/ ***

Unit 3

at *prep* /æt, ət/ ***
B & B *n* /ˌbiː ən ˈbiː/
bargain *n* /ˈbɑːɡɪn/ **
by (bus / plane / train) *phrase* /baɪ (ˈbʌs, ˈpleɪn, ˈtreɪn)/ ***
campsite *n* /ˈkæmpsaɪt/
comfortable *adj* /ˈkʌmftəbl/ ***
culture *n* /ˈkʌltʃə/ ***
deluxe *adj* /dɪˈlʌks/
distance *n* /ˈdɪstəns/ ***
exciting *adj* /ɪkˈsaɪtɪŋ/ **
exotic *adj* /ɪɡˈzɒtɪk/ *
five-star *adj* /ˈfaɪv ˌstɑː/
historical *adj* /hɪˈstɒrɪkl/ ***
home comforts *n pl* /ˌhəʊm ˈkʌmfəts/
in *prep* /ɪn/ ***
island *n* /ˈaɪlənd/ ***
lifestyle *n* /ˈlaɪfstaɪl/ **
luxury *adj* /ˈlʌkʃəri/ *
mountain *n* /ˈmaʊntɪn/ ***
nervous *adj* /ˈnɜːvəs/ **
on foot *phrase* /ˌɒn ˈfʊt/
physically *adv* /ˈfɪzɪkli/ **
pilgrim *n* /ˈpɪlɡrɪm/
pilgrimage *n* /ˈpɪlɡrɪmɪdʒ/
private villa *n* /ˌpraɪvət ˈvɪlə/
relaxing *adj* /rɪˈlæksɪŋ/
religion *n* /rɪˈlɪdʒən/ ***
resort *n* /rɪˈzɔːt/ *
self-catering apartment *n* /ˌself ˈkeɪtərɪŋ əˌpɑːtmənt/
shopping *n* /ˈʃɒpɪŋ/ **
sightseeing *n* /ˈsaɪtsiːɪŋ/
spiritual *adj* /ˈspɪrɪtʃuəl/ **
sunbathing *n* /ˈsʌnˌbeɪðɪŋ/
to *prep* /tuː, tə/ ***
traveller *n* /ˈtrævələ/ **
tropical paradise *n* /ˌtrɒpɪkl ˈpærədaɪs/
visiting museums *n* /ˌvɪzɪtɪŋ mjuːˈziːəmz/
white-water rafting *n* /ˌwaɪt ˌwɔːtə ˈrɑːftɪŋ/

Unit 4

angry *adj* /ˈæŋɡri/ ***
auction *n* /ˈɔːkʃn/ *
bid *n, v* /bɪd/ **
bored *adj* /bɔːd/ **
browse *v* /braʊz/ *
confident *adj* /ˈkɒnfɪdənt/ **
convenient *adj* /kənˈviːniənt/ **
designer *adj* /dɪˈzaɪnə/ **
disappointed *adj* /ˌdɪsəˈpɔɪntɪd/ *
exchange *v* /ɪksˈtʃeɪndʒ/ **
fake *adj* /feɪk/
fault *n* /fɔːlt/ ***
feedback *n* /ˈfiːdbæk/ **
healthy *adj* /ˈhelθi/ ***
helpful *adj* /ˈhelpfl/ **
in stock *phrase* /ˌɪn ˈstɒk/
in the sale *phrase* /ˌɪn ðə ˈseɪl/
insurance *n* /ɪnˈʃʊərəns/ ***
misunderstanding *n* /ˌmɪsʌndəˈstændɪŋ/ *
model *n* /ˈmɒdl/ ***
online *adv* /ˌɒnˈlaɪn/
patient *adj* /ˈpeɪʃnt/ **
polite *adj* /pəˈlaɪt/ *
public *adj* /ˈpʌblɪk/ ***
receipt *n* /rɪˈsiːt/ *
reduction *n* /rɪˈdʌkʃn/ ***
refund *n* /ˈriːfʌnd/
replace *v* /rɪˈpleɪs/ ***
review *n* /rɪˈvjuː/ ***
rude *adj* /ruːd/ **
shy *adj* /ʃaɪ/ *
suspicious *adj* /səˈspɪʃəs/ **
tip *n* /tɪp/ **
unhelpful *adj* /ʌnˈhelpfl/
unlimited *adj* /ʌnˈlɪmɪtɪd/ *
variety *n* /vəˈraɪəti/ ***
warranty *n* /ˈwɒrənti/

Communication activities

Unit 1, Lead-in Ex 3 page 66

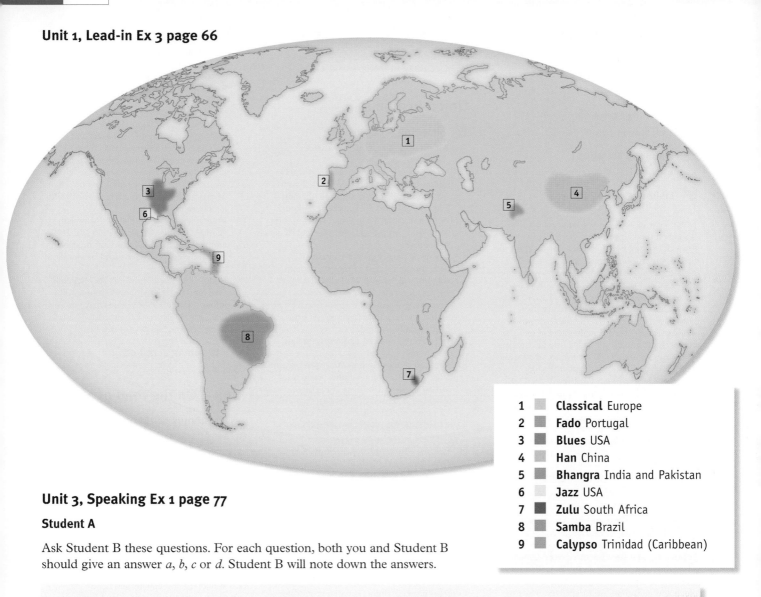

1 **Classical** Europe
2 **Fado** Portugal
3 **Blues** USA
4 **Han** China
5 **Bhangra** India and Pakistan
6 **Jazz** USA
7 **Zulu** South Africa
8 **Samba** Brazil
9 **Calypso** Trinidad (Caribbean)

Unit 3, Speaking Ex 1 page 77

Student A

Ask Student B these questions. For each question, both you and Student B should give an answer *a*, *b*, *c* or *d*. Student B will note down the answers.

What kind of **traveller** are you?

1 **Which of these places would you prefer to travel to?**
   a A resort in a tropical paradise with a great beach.
   b An exciting city in Europe.
   c An exotic place in a developing country.
   d Any place you can do your favourite sport (tennis, diving, skiing, swimming, etc.).

2 **If a friend invited you on one of these trips, which would you go on?**
   a To go white-water rafting on a big river.
   b To go and see the football World Cup final.
   c To stay at a deluxe resort in Fiji.
   d To go shopping and visit art galleries in Paris.

3 **Which of these four trips appeals most to you?**
   a Camping out with an Amazonian tribe.
   b Seeing the Terracotta Army in Xian, China.
   c Spending a week in Milan, Florence and Rome.
   d Going to Maui in Hawaii.

4 **If you had a free day during a business trip to Los Angeles, what would you do?**
   a Some kind of sport (tennis, scuba diving, etc.).
   b Go sightseeing.
   c Go shopping.
   d Go and lie on the beach.

5 **When a friend tells you about their trip, what is the first question you ask?**
   a What hotels and restaurants did you like best?
   b What did you see and do there?
   c What did you buy there?

Listening scripts

Unit 1 Get down to the rhythm

 Listening script 01

Lead-in Ex 1 from page 66

 Listening script 02

Reading text from page 67

 Listening script 03

Pronunciation Ex 2 from page 69

 Listening script 04

1

Every February we have a fantastic carnival. It's called the Carnevale d'Ivrea. Ivrea is my town. It's in the north of Italy, not far from the Swiss border. The carnival lasts for five days. This carnival has taken place every year since 1808, so it's been held for about 200 years. We have different teams, like armies. Everybody wears different costumes. There are the Devils, the Mercenaries, the Panthers, and many more. When the soldiers come into the city on their horses, we throw oranges at them, thousands of oranges. You have to take care – with more than 10,000 people throwing oranges, it's easy to get hit. Like in the French revolution, a red hat is the symbol of liberty, and everyone should wear one. If you don't, be careful because everyone will throw oranges at you. On the very last day of the carnival, we eat fish and fried polenta – oh, it's so delicious, and on the final evening we light huge bonfires in the town square. I recommend you go there if you are in Italy in February. You won't regret it.

2

We have Mardi Gras and the Music Festival in December, but my favourite festival is actually the Flower Festival. It takes place every February and it lasts for three days. Chiang Mai is Thailand's second city; it's called the Rose of the North because it's a beautiful place and in January and February, when the flowers blossom, it smells so good. The best part of the festival is the parade. Each float is decorated with flowers and on the top of each one is a contestant in the beauty contest, wearing traditional Thai clothes. The winner of the beauty contest is crowned the Flower Festival Queen. The first flower festival was held in 1977. We have held one every year since then. I usually go with my sister. We stand at the side of the road as the parade passes in front of us. The people in the parade hand out roses, orchids and lilies to the spectators, so we all go home with handfuls of sweet-smelling flowers.

3

When the Carnival first started in Notting Hill in 1964, it was a place where a lot of people from Trinidad lived. Now there are a lot of rich people living in Notting Hill, but for two days every August it becomes a little part of the Caribbean again. The festival is famous for its parade. There is an eight-kilometre route which goes all round west London. Hundreds of thousands of people come to watch the floats – you know, the decorated vehicles in the parade – with the people in their carnival costumes. Everybody loves the music, too. The music of the festival is calypso, the music of Trinidad. There are more than ten steel drum bands and they make sure the calypso never

stops. It's great to see so many people dancing in the street. When you come to the Notting Hill Festival, you have to try Jerk chicken – it's a spicy Caribbean speciality and it's delicious. See you next August.

Unit 2 Just do it

 Listening script 05

(I = Interviewer, S = Sam, Sp = Spider, M = Monkey)

I: I'm here on the streets of London with a group of young athletes. Are they here to play basketball? No, nothing so obvious. They are going to tell me about parkour. It's the fastest growing urban sport in the world. Sam, let me speak to you first. What is parkour?

S: Parkour is the art of free-running. We move through a part of the city without stopping. Like a river. You run, you jump, but you don't stop. You always move forwards, in harmony with everything around you. It's total freedom – it's the most beautiful feeling.

I: And have you played parkour for a long time, Sam?

S: Well, you don't play parkour – you play a game. Parkour is not a game, it's an art. You do parkour. I've done it for three years, but it started in Paris years ago. It's not new.

I: Spider, how long have you been doing parkour?

Sp: It all started when I was about ten. A friend dared me to jump off a balcony. I was like 'No way!' But this kid who was younger than me did it. So, because I was bigger than him, I did a more dangerous jump.

S: A lot of people think that parkour is all gymnastics and jumping off tall buildings. But that's only a small part of it.

I: I see. Monkey, what do you call someone who does parkour?

M: We call ourselves traceurs or free-runners.

I: Free runners? Right. Is parkour good for you?

M: Is it good for your health? Yeah, absolutely. I've never really been into sport – I prefer PlayStation to playing football – I was the fattest boy in my class. But since I started parkour, I've got really fit. I would say to anyone: If you want to do a sport, do parkour. It's better than any other sport.

I: But is it scarier than any other sport? Have you ever hurt yourself?

M: Not really. I hurt my foot once. Nothing special – that was the worst thing that's happened to me. Anyway, it's not as scary as going skiing or going scuba diving.

I: Last question, Sam. Why do you do it?

S: Because it's cool. Most of us do other sports as well, but parkour is more than just a sport, it's a way of life. And it's the easiest way for us to do exercise, get fit and feel totally free all at the same time. We're not stuck in a gym, we're out in the heart of the city.

 Listening script 06

I'm a bit fatter than my best friend, Tanya, but I'm still better than her at tennis. I just find it easier than she does, I suppose. Tanya's not as tall as I am, but she's very good-looking. She's more beautiful than any of the other women in our group, anyway.

 Listening script 07

1 On April 17, 2000 Australian Matt 'The Kangaroo Kid' Coulter jumped a distance of 40.9 m on his quad bike in Suffolk, England, earning him a place in the Guinness Book of Records.

2 Former NBA player Tyrone 'Muggsy' Bogues, is just 1.60 m tall. Despite his height, he was one of the fastest and most popular players on the NBA circuit.

3 Hawaiian-born Akebono became the first non-Japanese wrestler to reach the level of yokozuna, the highest rank in sumo wrestling. He is 2.4 m tall and weighs 235 kg. He retired in 2001.

4 French snowboarder Karine Ruby won six World Cup titles between 1996 and 2003 and has nearly 120 World Cup medals, 65 of them gold. No other snowboarder has achieved as much.

5 Eddie 'The Eagle' Edwards was Britain's first (and only) Olympic ski jumper. He jumped in the 1988 Winter Olympics in Calgary. He never won a medal. The only thing he came away with was bruises.

 Listening script 08

Reading text from page 72

Unit 3 On the road again

 Listening script 09

Reading text from page 74

Listening script 10

(I = Interviewer)

Omar

I: Where do you like going on holiday?

O: Everywhere. Anywhere. It must be exciting, though. I can't stand doing nothing. I need action to keep me interested. I love travelling. I've been to all five continents and visited more than sixty countries.

I: Where do you usually stay?

O: On a campsite if I can. I love camping – the feeling that you're sleeping under the stars with just a tent to cover you. It's not always possible to camp, so I rent an apartment – but always self-catering, so that I can cook my own food.

I: And what do you do during the day?

O: On my last holiday I went white-water rafting down the Zambezi River in Zambia. Extreme, but the Victoria Falls were absolutely incredible.

Serena

I: What is your ideal holiday destination?

S: Well, I spend the rest of the year working hard, so I prefer to go somewhere relaxing. I guess my ideal place would be some tropical paradise where I don't have to lift a finger. I can just chill out.

I: Where do you prefer to stay?

S: I only get the chance to take a break once a year from my busy life, so I usually stay in a resort. Everything is paid for: food, accommodation, drinks … all I need to do is relax.

I: And what do you usually do with your time?

S: I usually spend my days sunbathing by the pool with a cool drink in one hand and a good book in the other.

Darren

I: Which type of place do you like going to?

D: Well, I haven't actually been anywhere as yet, but I'd want to go somewhere exotic. It would have to be somewhere with top quality service. Only the best. Everything deluxe. You know what I mean?

I: And what type of place would you like to stay in?

D: I could see myself in a private villa in the Maldives, with servants. You know, all the home comforts.

I: And what would you do during the day?

D: Nothing.

Rebecca

R: It's not really important where I go. And as far as accommodation is concerned, I usually stay in a two-star hotel – that's always good enough for me. I prefer to spend my money on other things.

I: And what do you usually do with your time?

R: I like shopping. I mean I really like shopping. I especially enjoy finding clothes that I can't get hold of at home. And I love picking up bargains – the cheaper the better. It feels great when you go home and people say, 'What a lovely top,' and I say, 'Yeah, and it only cost £5 – bargain!' I don't know which I love more, paying so little or seeing the faces of my friends when I tell them.

Jun

I: Where do you like going to on holiday?

J: I always try to travel to a country or city with plenty to see and do. I love historical cities like Moscow, Paris and my favourite, Kyoto, in Japan.

I: What type of accommodation do you choose?

J: I usually stay in a B & B, a bed and breakfast, as they are cheaper than hotels.

I: And what do you usually do?

J: I spend my days sightseeing – visiting all the famous places – oh, and I love visiting museums. It's so wonderful for me, you know, to walk around and find out about the customs of the local people.

Unit 4 Out and about

 Listening script 11

(S = Shop assistant, P = Paula)

S: Can I help you?

P: Yes, I bought this printer a short time ago, and I'm having trouble with it already.

S: What seems to be the problem?

P: Sometimes it just stops printing half way through. Not every time, but frequently. It's very annoying. I'd like a refund, please.

S: Do you have a receipt?

P: Yes, here it is.

S: I'm sorry, you bought this five weeks ago. We can only give you your money back if the item is less than one month old.

P: But it's been breaking down since I bought it. I didn't do anything to it. I think there's a fault in the machine.

S: Once again, I can only say I'm sorry to hear about your printer. There is a one-year warranty on it. I'm sure the maker would agree to replace it. Why don't you call them and explain the situation?

P: Can't I just exchange it here?

S: I'm afraid that model is no longer in stock. It's not very reliable.

P: Now you tell me. I think I'll shop online next time. It's cheaper and more convenient. And now that I have to wait for the maker to send me a machine, it's exactly the same as buying online.

S: Yes. Is there anything else I can help you with?

P: Like you helped me with this? I don't think so, thank you. Goodbye.

S: Thank you. Goodbye.

 Listening script 12

Reading text from page 79

 Listening script 13

It's fun to dream about what I'd do if I had lots of money. I'd buy a Ferrari if I could choose the car of my dreams. If I had a Ferrari, I'd drive it straight to the shops. I'd spend hours buying designer clothes, if I was in the right mood. Then, if I had time, I'd go for a coffee with my A-list celebrity friends. At the end of the day, if I felt like staying in, I'd have a long, relaxing bath before going to bed.

Unit 5 Review

 Listening script 14

Song from page 84

Listening script 15

A: Excuse me. Can I ask you a few questions for a shopping survey?

B: Yes, of course.

A: How old are you?

B: I'm 26.

A: What do you do?

B: I'm a computer programmer.

A: Hm-mm. Do you have a credit card?

B: Yes, I do.

A: How long have you had it?

B: I've had it for about three years.

A: How often do you go shopping?

B: Mm. I usually go every weekend. I love shopping.

A: Where would you go shopping if you could afford it?

B: I'd go to Paris if I had the opportunity. There are some wonderful designer shops in Paris.

Communication activities

Unit 3, Speaking Ex 1 page 77

Student B

1   Student A is going to ask you some questions. For each question, tick *a*, *b*, *c* or *d* in 'What kind of traveller are you?' for yourself and for Student A.

2   Find the traveller type (Adventurer, Sports lover, etc.) that is listed the most for the answers you gave. This is your traveller type. For example, if you have ticked 'Sports lover' more times than any other traveller type, then you are a Sports lover! (It's possible to be more than one traveller type.)

3   Tell Student A what his / her traveller type is and read the explanation. Do you agree with the results?

What kind of traveller are you?

		My answer	A's answer	
1	a	☐	☐	Relaxer
	b	☐	☐	Shopper, Comfort seeker
	c	☐	☐	Adventurer, Culture lover
	d	☐	☐	Sports lover
2	a	☐	☐	Adventurer
	b	☐	☐	Sports lover
	c	☐	☐	Comfort seeker, Relaxer
	d	☐	☐	Shopper, culture lover
3	a	☐	☐	Adventurer
	b	☐	☐	Culture lover
	c	☐	☐	Shopper
	d	☐	☐	Sports lover, Comfort seeker, Relaxer
4	a	☐	☐	Sports lover
	b	☐	☐	Adventurer, Culture lover
	c	☐	☐	Shopper
	d	☐	☐	Comfort seeker, Relaxer
5	a	☐	☐	Comfort seeker, Relaxer
	b	☐	☐	Sports lover, Adventurer, Culture lover
	c	☐	☐	Shopper

traveller types

Adventurer Adventurers just live for the next experience. You probably began travelling when you were young and now you can't live without it. You also love physical challenge or physical risk. It is not enough for you to see the Grand Canyon's Colorado River, you'd have to go white-water rafting on it.

Sports lover Sports lovers may have no interest in travel but you love spending your holidays doing your favourite sport (wind surfing, skiing, etc.). You don't even have do a sport; it's enough just to watch with other sports fans. You are always the first to make reservations for major sports events.

Relaxer Most relaxers want to spend their holidays doing absolutely nothing. You are probably in business and you work long hours and never get enough sleep. Or you may be a busy parent who wants time away from the kids. Your ideal holiday spot is a resort where you don't have to lift a finger.

Comfort seeker You wouldn't think of leaving home, unless it was to go to a deluxe hotel with perfect service. Your excitement is not where you go but how you go. You may just want what's normal for you – the best. Or maybe you are a normal person who wants to enjoy the luxury you can't have every day.

Culture lover Culture lovers travel to learn about the people, customs and maybe language of another culture. You usually prefer to stay in one city or country for a couple of weeks or more. You enjoy meeting people, shopping in local markets, visiting museums and sightseeing.

Shopper Most travellers spend some time picking up bargains that they can't find at home or getting souvenirs for family and friends. Shoppers, by contrast, travel to shop. Anything else you do on holiday, you do when the shops are closed.